Columbia University

Contributions to Education

Teachers College Series

No. 684

AMS PRESS

NEW YORK

PROVISIONS FOR GENERAL THEORY COURSES IN THE PROFESSIONAL EDUCATION OF TEACHERS

BY

OBED JALMAR WILLIAMSON, Ph.D.

TEACHERS COLLEGE, COLUMBIA UNIVERSITY
CONTRIBUTIONS TO EDUCATION, No. 684

Published with the Approval of
Professor R. B. Raup, Sponsor

BUREAU OF PUBLICATIONS
Teachers College, Columbia University
NEW YORK CITY
1936

Library of Congress Cataloging in Publication Data

Williamson, Obed Jalmar, 1899-
 Provisions for general theory courses in the professional education of teachers.

 Reprint of the 1936 ed., issued in series: Teachers
College, Columbia University. Contributions to educa-
tion, no. 684.
 Originally presented as the author's thesis,
Columbia.
 Bibliography: p.
 1. Education--Study and teaching. 2. Teachers,
Training of--Curricula. 3. Education--Philosophy.
I. Title. II. Series: Columbia University.
Teachers College. Contributions to education, no. 684.
LB1731.W47 1972   370'.732   78-177634
ISBN 0-404-55684-1

Reprinted by Special Arrangement with Teachers
College Press, New York, New York

From the edition of 1936, New York
First AMS edition published in 1972
Manufactured in the United States

AMS PRESS, INC.
NEW YORK, N. Y.   10003

7.85

ACKNOWLEDGMENTS

To Professor R. B. Raup, the sponsor of this dissertation, the writer is greatly indebted; he gave generously of his time and counsel. The other members of the committee, Professors W. C. Bagley and Harold Rugg made many valuable suggestions and stimulating criticisms. The author wishes also to acknowledge the valuable assistance given by Professors W. H. Kilpatrick, John L. Childs, and Donald P. Cottrell. Their constructive criticisms of the manuscript and their help throughout the writer's sojourn at Teachers College are greatly appreciated.

The writer also wishes to express gratitude to Dr. Francis Peterson of the University of Hawaii, who collaborated with him in the investigation which formed the basis of this study. This contact with Dr. Peterson enhanced the quality of this work and enriched the life of the writer.

Dr. Manly H. Harper gave many valuable suggestions in the preparation of the chief instrument used in this study and in the subsequent analysis of the data. In the preparation of the manuscript the author wishes to acknowledge valuable help from Dr. M. Grossman and Dr. H. D. Langford.

Most of all, he is indebted to his wife, Ruth Guss Williamson, not only for inspiration and encouragement, but for valuable help throughout the study; she has been a partner in the real sense of the term.

O. J. W.

CONTENTS

CHAPTER I

INTRODUCTION

THE type of course in the professional curriculum for teachers with which this study is concerned can best be understood by first viewing the curriculum as a whole. At present there is great variation among the various normal schools, teachers colleges, and departments of education at universities and liberal arts colleges, but roughly the courses can be classified into four distinct classes.

One group includes the subject-matter courses such as English or mathematics. These courses are taught chiefly for two purposes: to develop a cultural background and to develop familiarity with subjects the candidate will teach. A second group may be characterized as the educational science group. This group of courses aims to give the prospective teacher an understanding of those scientific data, hypotheses, theories, and laws upon which present educational practice is based and by which educational procedures may be improved. Teaching, like any art, is based wherever possible upon scientific principles. To discover these principles has been the function of educational psychology, educational physiology, and educational sociology. Still another group of courses aims at equipping the prospective teacher with the technical procedures necessary for the practice of education. In this group are the courses in special methods and sometimes even general method, and courses in the techniques of testing and measuring intelligence and educational achievement. Courses in educational administration, school management, and educational statistics are also included in this group.

Finally, there is the type of course with which this study is concerned—courses which deal with educational theory.[1] The courses

---

[1] In this study general educational theory and philosophy of education will be used synonymously. The word theory is used with a conscious recognition of the fact that it is not a satisfactory word. It is objectionable because it is often used in connection with science or hypothesis. It is recognized that theory and philosophy do not mean the same thing. For example, theory of medicine connotes the science—physiology, anatomy—on which medicine is based, while philosophy of medicine connotes the broader aspects of the profession such as professional ethics or an attitude toward socialized medicine. If the term philosophy of edu-

included in this group are those that have as their purpose the developing of a broad view of life and of education. They aim to open up the considerations upon which desirable educational aims and practices are to be based, and to make explicit the viewpoints and biases that determine procedures.

The most typical general educational theory course is principles of education, or philosophy of education as it is sometimes called. Although this course occasionally deals with topics not directly of a theoretical nature, such as administrative procedures or the techniques of teaching and testing, in its most common form it deals with such broad and general problems as aims and objectives, moral education, broad problems of cultural and vocational education, and the relationship of church, home, and other educational agencies to the school and to each other. This course in its purest form has sought to equip the teacher with principles and generalizations which give him orientation and direction for dealing with questions of teaching procedure.

There are, in addition to philosophy or principles of education, a number of other courses whose primary purpose is not the development of a guiding philosophy of education, but which frequently include material of a broadly theoretical nature. Introduction to education is of this type. Its main purpose, as the title suggests, is to introduce the student to the profession of education by discussing the advantages and disadvantages of teaching as a life career, by presenting some of the most elementary principles of psychology, methods of teaching, school administration, and frequently by including brief summaries of the history of education. In addition, this course usually includes some consideration of the aims of education, its place in society, the function of the teacher. To the extent the course is concerned with such broader topics, it is a course in general educational theory.

Another course of this type is one which deals with those teaching procedures common to most of the school subjects, such as the art of questioning, making the assignment, maintaining class discipline, and is variously called principles of teaching, technique of teaching, or general method. Besides presenting general teaching procedures, it often deals with such broader problems as aims and

___

cation were used solely, it might be understood as referring only to the course, philosophy of education. By using the term general educational theory this difficulty is eliminated because it is not limited to any one course.

objectives of education and moral education. [95][2] In the degree that this course is confined to teaching procedures, it comes within the category of the techniques courses mentioned above; to the extent that it attempts to view the broad problems of life in formulating an educational program, it is properly to be thought of as a general educational theory course.

History of education as sometimes taught should be included as a general theory course—especially when it deals with the basic educational philosophies of educational reformers and the evolution of educational theory. Educational sociology may at times be taught as a general theory course, but again this course is difficult to classify. In so far as it attempts to place education within the full social context, it is educational theory. In so far as it aims at giving data and principles to be accepted and not to be criticized as guides for educational programs and procedures, it falls within the area of educational science courses. [97]

No hard and fast line can be drawn between courses in educational science, educational techniques, and general educational theory. Occasionally one chances upon a catalogue description of a methods course which indicates that the course devotes considerable attention to theory as described above. On the other hand, one is just as likely to come across a course in principles of education which limits itself to "scientific" data and theories culled from the fields of administration, statistics, and psychology used in the procedures of education. Sometimes the principles course is even more limited in considering only teaching techniques. The category in which a particular course falls depends on the teacher, his outlook, the textbook, and the topics discussed.

To state it differently, courses in general educational theory, and principles of education in particular, are not appropriately concerned with the mere technique of teaching the various school subjects— the teaching of long division, for example. They are not directly concerned with the techniques of testing educational achievement nor with statistical computation. They are not concerned with mere descriptions of psychological or sociological phenomena. They are not concerned with the techniques of school administration or classroom management. They are, rather, concerned with the broad considerations upon which the use of the above named techniques are based. A study of general educational theory should give the stu-

[2] Throughout this study, numbers in brackets refer to references in the Bibliography.

dent such a unified outlook on life that he can see things in life, society, and education in their interrelationships, and more particularly the place of education as a social function. Such a study should clarify the nature of the good life and the good society.

Inasmuch as principles or philosophy of education is usually more completely devoted to a consideration of these theoretical problems and to the development of a broad point of view than are the other general education courses mentioned above, chief emphasis in this study will be devoted to this course. The findings will of course be applicable to the teaching of general educational theory wherever it appears, but the purposes of this study will best be served by confining our attention mainly to the course in principles or philosophy of education.

Present social conditions require that a study into the teaching of general educational theory be made. The chaos and confusion that prevail in society today have so upset inherited beliefs that a revaluation of aims and procedures seems unavoidable. [93 : I-II] Principles, assumptions, and ideas once taken for granted, now are questioned. Wherever one looks in society today, confusion and uncertainty are to be found. In the sphere of economics the theory of *laissez faire* is being countered by the practice and theory of social control. In government three theories are fighting for control—democracy, communism, and fascism. The field of religion presents a maze of conflicting beliefs, and inherited creeds are being discarded with ever greater willingness. At no time in the history of the world has unrest, dislocation, and utter confusion been so widespread and so deep-seated.

This confusion which seems to be unsettling the very foundations of civilization has also upset complacency in education. The apparent necessity of social reconstruction makes imperative a redefining of the function of the school. There is a growing realization that the theories on which the school was based in the past are no longer adequate and that the new social demands require a modification of these theories. Educational objectives, once taken for granted and memorized by students of education, are now held in doubt and many have even been discarded. Where once there were certainty and finality, now the most characteristic attitude is uncertainty. The "science of education," which began to assume a position of certainty and power, is now weakening because the very assumptions upon which it was based are called into question. In other words, confusion in society is reflected in the school and in educational theory. It is becoming more and more evident that if the school is to adjust to a rapidly changing society it must re-think and re-construct its determining theories. A study of the courses which deal with theory should reveal their applicability or their lack of applicability to the peculiar social conditions which today prevail.

A study of courses in general educational theory is appropriate for other reasons. These courses have been forced into attention by the criticism aimed at them in teacher-training circles. Especially is this true in the case of principles of education. The charge has been made that it is "too vague," and "too theoretical." Times without number the writer has heard this course referred to as "the bunk," "a waste of time," and "a snap course." It is frequently held that today, with a great science of education and of psychology, there is little need for philosophical considerations. It is urged that teaching success depends upon the mastery of teaching techniques secured through scientific experimentation and the techniques of achievement and intelligence testing. Some educators are saying that the vague speculations of general educational theory courses can make little contribution to the professional equipment of the modern teacher. They are urging a reduction of time to be devoted to these courses or that they be eliminated altogether.

This situation is the more serious in view of the fact that all teacher-training institutions give and usually require courses in general educational theory. State certificating agencies, too, often specify courses of this type. Various studies of teacher-training curricula show that most institutions offer and sometimes require several courses dealing with general theory, courses which often carry from three to five hours' credit. This means that whether or not they are of value in preparing teachers for their work, they do consume considerable time and effort on the part of students and instructors.

This study, then, aims to examine the rôle which general educational theory, especially as found in principles or philosophy of education, plays in the education of teachers. Since the present teaching of general educational theory is an outgrowth of the past, the history or the teaching of general theory in teacher-training institutions will be delineated with particular reference to those aspects that bear on present problems. The study aims to discover the relative importance of general theory, the kind of theory taught, and the adequacy of the content of theory courses. It aims to investigate the education and experience of the instructors of these courses and their attitudes toward certain educational and social issues. Finally, on the basis of the findings, recommendations will be made as to the function and importance of courses in general educational theory in professional curricula for teachers.

For the purpose of examining the teaching of general educational theory in the light of the developing social and educational situation, the writer has drawn freely from material in American history and especially the history of education. Studies of the origin and development of teacher-training institutions in the United States, of the curricula of these institutions at different periods in their history, textbooks in the field of education, and yearbooks of various educational organizations were examined. Throughout the writer has attempted to discover those aspects of the social scene and those elements in the various educational philosophies that have stimulated the writing and teaching of general educational theory. Of great value in orienting the writer with respect to problems in the teaching of educational theory and certain aspects of the evolution of such courses have been the numerous interviews and conferences with professors of Teachers College, Columbia University, and the School of Education at New York University and graduate students at Teachers College who have been engaged in the teaching of general courses in education.

With the end in view of discovering the relative importance attributed to courses in general educational theory in the total program of teacher preparation and the trends and the tendencies toward change in regard to this field, a number of studies dealing with the curricula of teacher-training institutions and with the development of certain courses in the teacher-training programs within the past few decades have been examined. To determine present content of the courses, some of the more recent of these studies were used together with an examination of catalogue descriptions of courses in principles or philosophy of education of sixty institutions engaged in the professional preparation of teachers, and an examination of some of the textbooks in this field.

For the purpose of conducting this study, two instruments have been devised by the writer, in collaboration with Dr. Francis Peterson and Professor R. B. Raup. [102][3] One consisted of a questionnaire; the other of a set of seventy-nine propositions. Both these instruments were sent to teachers of education in twenty-five teacher-

[3] A copy of each of these instruments will be found in the Appendix.

training institutions in the spring of 1931.[4] The questionnaire included among others a number of direct questions in response to which the teachers were to indicate their attitudes toward the courses in general theory given in their institutions, what degree of importance they ascribed to these courses in the training of teachers, and the criticism they had to offer with respect to them. Among the propositions in the second instrument were a number that were devised for the purpose of eliciting the teachers' views on the value of general theory. Responses from 551 instructors were obtained, fifty-six of whom were engaged in the teaching of courses in general theory.

The main purpose of the instruments was to elicit information about the training and experience of the instructors in educational theory and to obtain data which might be helpful in arriving at a picture about their educational philosophies. The questionnaire served the purpose of obtaining data about their training and experience. The list of seventy-nine propositions was devised for the purpose of bringing to the surface the philosophies of education of the teachers.[5] Hereafter the seventy-nine propositions will be referred to as the "instrument."

For the purpose of discovering the social philosophies of the instructors a third instrument was used, Harper's *A Social Study* [87].[6] The "instrument" and Harper's were used on the assumption that what the instructor does in the classroom depends very much upon his own beliefs about education, the individual, society, and life in general.

[4] These institutions were located as follows: teachers colleges and normal schools —Pennsylvania, 3; New York, 4; New Jersey, 3; Massachusetts, 2; and 1 each in Illinois, Michigan, Connecticut, Maryland; liberal arts colleges—Pennsylvania, 9.

[5] The instrument was prepared primarily for use in the National Survey of the Education of Teachers conducted by the United States Office of Education.

[6] A copy of this instrument is to be found in the Appendix.

CHAPTER II

THE ORIGIN AND DEVELOPMENT OF COURSES IN GENERAL EDUCATIONAL THEORY

THE task of this study is an appraisal of the present status and content of courses in general educational theory in the light of the pertinent facts and problems of the present social situation. No such appraisal is wholly possible without an insight into the origin and development of the teaching of educational theory. Such an insight will not only serve the purpose of illustrating the dynamic relations between the subject matter of general educational theory and the shifting social scene, but will also be of aid in discriminating between those strands in general theory and its teaching which have a vital function in the present educational and social pattern and those which are merely survivals of the past. It is in view of this consideration that this chapter seeks to describe the first efforts to teach general educational theory and the subsequent development of courses in the general theory of education. Inasmuch as the history of teaching of general theory is inextricably bound up with the history of educational theory itself, the discussion will include some exposition of the development of educational thought. An effort will be made to view the history of general theory teaching in the context of the changing provisions for teacher training. Only so much of the treatment of general educational theory and the provisions for teacher training as is essential for the understanding of the development of the teaching of theoretical courses in education will be included.

The historical background of present-day teaching of educational theory can be conveniently considered in the light of certain tendencies which eventuated in the emergence of important new patterns of educational thought and practice. Up to 1860 little critical reflection concerning the aims and methods of education is discernible. Both were based on inherited values and experiences and on new motifs introduced by democracy, nationalism, and opportunities for material gain. Here and there echoes of the Pestalozzian spirit influenced school procedure, but it was not until the sixties that

Pestalozzianism—in a garbled form—came to. be a dominant force in shaping the contour of American education. By 1880 the impetus of object teaching had exhausted itself and new influences introduced somewhat earlier had become dominant factors in a new reconstruction of education. Like Pestalozzianism these influences, too, were European in their origin. Froebelian, Hegelian, and Herbartian ideas came to constitute the mold in which new practices were formed. The reign of what might be variously termed metaphysical, transcendental, absolutist ideas in education remained uncontested until the turn of the twentieth century. By the middle of the first decade of the twentieth century serious contenders in the shape of the scientific movement and the development of American pragmatism appeared upon the scene.

An effort will be made to delineate the salient characteristics of the teaching of general theory of education in each of these periods and to indicate the chief points of emphasis.

SECTION I

ESTABLISHMENT OF PROFESSIONALIZED TEACHER EDUCATION AND THE TEACHING OF GENERAL EDUCATIONAL THEORY

Institutions for the professional education of teachers are of comparatively recent origin. None existed in this country until the third decade of the nineteenth century and even at that late date the country was very slow to see the need for providing professional education for its teachers.

The goal which was set before education and the contents of the educational program were such as seemingly to render professional education for teachers unnecessary. The central motif of New England civilization during the Colonial times was religion. The aim of life was to attain salvation of the individual soul. Education was largely subservient to this interest and aim. The teacher who succeeded in enabling the pupils to read the Bible—the sole means of salvation—in eliciting rote answers to the questions in the catechism, and in fixing a few simple arithmetical skills was considered successfully to have accomplished his task. [20:II] Obviously to accomplish this comparatively simple educational objective, there was little need for professionally trained teachers. Anyone who could read, who was "strong in the faith," who could discipline children in the pious virtues, could teach. Consequently most of the teachers were persons closely connected with the church and, for the older pupils, often clergymen.[1]

But forces were at work at the turn of the century to change this simple conception of education and ultimately to make imperative professional education for teachers. Democracy originating in the English tradition and reinforced by the spirit of the French enlightenment, and the frontier experience; the rising tide of nationalism released by the Revolutionary War and heightened by the War of 1812; and the spirit of individualism fostered by the presence of a continent to be conquered and exploited have all coöperated in the expansion of the sphere of education and in the transformation of its spirit, content, and aims. [72:IV]

Education began to assume a larger rôle in the lives of the people. The fact that a representative democracy makes education more necessary became ever more clear to the leaders. Jefferson, Franklin, and other liberal thinkers of the period proposed plans for an American system of schools which would teach the principles of representative democracy, develop loyalty to America, and foster American culture. They insisted that a republic of illiterate and unenlightened citizens could not continue to exist. They believed that "education and political reform were inseparable." They went further to insist that the school was the chief agency for reforming society and for humanizing the lives of the underprivileged classes.

The political agitation incident to the Revolution had generated interest in law, history, and government. With the launching of the new republic, the aim of developing understanding of the civic responsibilities involved became increasingly important. A demand was made for teaching history and geography. In 1786 Benjamin Rush, one of several who prepared a national plan for education, wrote: "Above all, let our youth be instructed in the history of the ancient republics and the progress of liberty and tyranny in the different states of Europe." [86:I-II]

---

[1] The following quotation indicates the importance of religion in the qualifications of teachers of that period: "He must be one that takes a lively interest in, and helps to build up the Christian Church; and must also be a God-fearing virtuous man, and lead an exemplary life, and must himself be a lover of the Word of God, and be diligent in its use as much as possible, among the children of the school; and he must set a good example, especially before the young children, and must avoid exhibitions of anger. He shall willingly and heartily seek to fulfill the duties obligatory upon him, with love to God and to the children; to the performance of which the Lord, their Maker, and Jesus, their Redeemer, have so strongly bound him." [113:141]

Thus the purpose of education was expanded. The religious motive began to give way to the social, democratic, and national motive. A further expansion took place under the influence of a desire for material competence. Mundane utility took place along with salvation as a goal to be achieved through education. Education clearly became an asset in the effort to gain wealth. In its turn increased material wealth gave rise to a demand for education richer in content than was customary in earlier and more primitive times. Wealth also made the fulfilment of the demand economically possible.

These forces which were changing the school, adding to its importance, expanding its functions so as to call into being professional teacher education, were augmented by a new influence which began to make itself felt in refining school practice. Pestalozzian theories and practices made their appearance upon the scene of American education. William Maclure's articles in 1806 in the *National Intelligencer* constitute the spearhead of Pestalozzianism on the American continent. [71 : 389-94] The work of Joseph Neef, a disciple of Pestalozzi brought to this country by Maclure to establish the new type of school, and of John Keagy in Harrisburg and Philadelphia, and the frequent reports by European visitors about the Yverdon, Stanz, and Burgdorf institutions helped to familiarize America with Pestalozzi. Pestalozzi had shown the necessity of studying the educative process. Teaching was not a simple matter of assigning portions of pages to be memorized and of then holding the book while the child repeated the passage. Teaching was described as a process of so directing the child in the unfolding of his latent powers that a "harmoniously" developed individual with all his "faculties" developed to the highest point was the result. This meant the teacher must understand child nature; he must know how to utilize the powers possessed by the child; he must know how to use the natural environment and how to arrange the school environment so the most effective and economical learning could be achieved. To get the child to learn he could not rely on brute force; he must use psychological methods.

Not only did Pestalozzi's work tend to expand the purposes of education and to psychologize the methods thereby indicating the necessity of teacher training, but his schools, especially his Teacher's Institute at Yverdon, served as patterns for the normal schools later to be established in Europe and America. The influence of Pestalozzi is further reflected in early textbooks used in education courses later to be described.

Another factor which encouraged the establishment of teacher-training institutions was the growing realization that the common schools had not kept pace with the material advancement of the country. The more intelligent people became aware of the fact that public education was of a very poor quality and that the teachers were inadequately prepared. Even in New England with its "public school tradition" education frequently languished. Ignorant and poorly trained teachers attempted to "keep school" in dilapidated buildings with practically no equipment. [104:366] Pen and voice became more articulate in demanding better schools. The obvious incompetence of the teachers called for some special provision for the education of teachers.[2]

Conditions were thus ripe for the advent of professional teacher education when in 1823 Samuel Reed Hall, a Congregational minister, established a school for the preparation of teachers at Concord, Vermont. [84:11-3] The curriculum was identical with that of the academy except that Hall gave a series of "lectures on school-keeping" for those who intended to teach.

Hall's work attracted so much attention that he was called to Phillips Andover Academy to teach his famous course at first called "art of teaching," later changed to "principles of teaching." By 1834 there were five academies in New York State offering "principles of teaching," the chief text for which was Hall's lectures published in book form. The same year the state legislature of New York passed an act (the first of its kind) making provision for the professional education of teachers to be carried on in certain selected academies. The program of courses, drawn up by a committee of the board of regents, included all the common branches and in addition a course in "moral and intellectual philosophy" and one in "principles of teaching." For the latter Hall's *Lectures on School-Keeping* was recommended. Other writings in the field of professional education were by this time available and were recommended for use in this course. They were Taylor's *The District School*, Abbott's *The Teacher*, and a magazine called *Annals of Education*, edited by William C. Woodbridge. [95:41-2, 99:40-2]

The next step in the development of professional education in the United States was the establishment of state-supported normal

[2] This feeling was well expressed by Governor Clinton of New York State, who in advocating professional education for teachers in the academies said it was important "that the mind and morals of the rising and perhaps the destinies of all future generations be not intrusted to the guardianship of incompetence."

schools. Hall's attempt at Concord and the efforts of the New York academies to prepare teachers must have been factors influencing this significant step. Certain also it is that the superb system of state education in Prussia with its provision for teacher training was among the influences leading to the establishment of state institutions for the training of teachers. [84:III][3] After considerable agitation and hard work on the part of James G. Carter and Horace Mann, the first state normal school in America was finally opened at Lexington, Mass., July 3, 1839. Here again we have evidence of the influence of Hall, for he had had close personal contact with both Carter and Mann. The result was that this first state normal school bore a close resemblance to Hall's schools at Concord, Vermont, and Phillips Andover, the chief difference being that the emphasis was placed on mastery of the subjects taught in the elementary school rather than the ordinary subjects of the academy, whereas in Hall's schools the curriculum was entirely on the secondary school level. The precedent of weekly lectures on "school-keeping" established by Hall was followed in this institution. The lectures were delivered by the principal who was believed to be a "master pedagogue." Out of his practical experience he would discuss methods of teaching, management of schools, the value of education. Materials to supplement these lectures were extremely meager—little beyond the writings of Hall, Taylor, and Abbott. [99:50-4]

Some conception of the nature of this course may be gained from a letter written by Cyrus Peirce, the first principal of the Lexington Normal School, a part of which is here quoted:

Two things I have aimed at, especially in this school. 1. To teach thoroughly the principles of the several branches studied, so that the pupils may have a clear understanding of them. 2. To teach the pupils, by my own example, as well as by precepts, the best way of teaching the same things effectually to others. I have four different methods of recitation. 1st, by question and answer; 2nd, by conversation; 3d, by calling on one, two, three, more or less, to give an analysis of the whole subject contained in the lesson; and 4th, by requiring written analyses, in which the ideas of the author are stated in the language of the pupil. . . . I am ever mingling or attempting to mingle, at these exercises, theory and example; frequently putting the inquiry to them, . . . "How would you express such and such a sentiment, or explain such a principle, or illustrate such a position to a class, which you may be teaching?"

[3] Some educational historians insist that professional education for teachers is entirely an American idea. Others with Gordy urge that the American normal school was the result of Prussian influence.

"Let me," I say to them, "hear your statements or witness your modes of illustrating and explaining." . . . Besides delivering to the school a written Formal Lecture once a week, in which I speak of the qualification, motives, and duties of teachers, the discipline, management, and instruction of schools, and the manner in which the various branches should be taught, I am every day, in conversations or a familiar sort of lectures, taking up and discussing more particularly and minutely, some point or points suggested by the exercises or occurrences, it may be, of the day relating to the internal operations of the schoolroom, as to physical, moral, or intellectual education. . . . I am constantly calling up real or supposed cases, and either asking the pupils what they would do in such a case or stating to them what I would do myself, or both. As a specimen of such questions, take the following, viz.: "On going into a school as a teacher, what is the first thing you would do? . . . What method will you adopt to teach spelling, reading, arithmetic? . . . What will you do if your scholars quarrel? Lie? Swear?" [128]

Thus it appears that early normal schools made but little provision for professional training of teachers. Whatever of it was undertaken had to be accomplished within one hour per week. In these circumstances little attention to theory could be expected. The emphasis was entirely on thoroughness in subject matter and mastery of specific teaching procedure for which practice teaching was provided. No widespread departure from this program can be noted until the sixties. Kruse notes that the plan of the Lexington school served as a model for all schools established in the forties and fifties. [95:44-5] Thus the Millersville Normal School established as late as 1859 was satisfied with only one course of lectures on education —"lectures on teaching." [11:136] Even such an educational pioneer as Horace Mann felt that the first business of the normal school consisted in "reviewing thoroughly and critically mastering the rudiments or elementary branches of knowledge." [84:44] Little value of theory was recognized in teacher training.

Within the period under consideration the only departure among state normal schools along lines of greater provision for professional training is to be noted in the case of the Albany Normal School founded in 1844. [95:46] David Perkins Page, the principal, was not satisfied with a review of the common branches and weekly lectures on teaching. He believed a professional course must have a professional curriculum and that the study of educational problems should occupy as important a place in the curriculum as any other course. It is to Page's influence that the growth in number and importance of professional courses is in a considerable degree due.

[124,95:46] This was accompanied by a growing emphasis on general educational theory.

What rôle did general theory play in the preparation of teachers? Some insight may be afforded by an examination of the textbooks then in use. The books were few in number, the most common of them being: *Lectures on School Keeping* by Samuel R. Hall (1829), *The District School* by J. O. Taylor (1834), *The Teacher* by Jacob Abbott (1837), *The Teacher's Manual* by Thomas H. Palmer (1840), *School and Schoolmaster* by Alonzo Potter and G. B. Emerson (1842), *Theory and Practice of Teaching* by David P. Page (1847), *Confessions of a Schoolmaster* by William A. Alcott (1856).

It is not the intention here to present a complete report of the educational philosophy of the period, but rather to point to those factors within it which most directly throw light on the problem with which we are dealing. The examination of these books was undertaken with the belief that the nature and the motives operative in the teaching of general educational theory of those times would best be seen in the broader conceptions which were advanced through writing and teaching. They reveal at one and the same time the prevailing philosophies and the corresponding sense of the needs of the teacher.

In general it can be stated that there was little conscious recognition of the need for a general theory of education. As far as classroom procedures are concerned the consensus seems to be that "experience," i.e., rule of thumb plus such discoveries as might haphazardly be hit upon, was quite sufficient. With respect to aims of education current at the time—piety, democracy, and material success —their meaning was so clear and their acceptance was so common that many educators were completely unconscious of them although they were implicit in their practice.

Obviously all of the books listed could not be described in detail. The discussion will limit itself to the three most popular books [94:328]: Hall's *Lectures on School Keeping*, Abbott's *The Teacher*, and Page's *Theory and Practice of Teaching*, the last the most significant because it marks a transition to a more mature theoretical foundation of education.

As has already been observed Hall's book was based on his lectures at Concord and Phillips Andover and was intended to furnish a complete course in education; whatever a teacher needed to know about education in both its general and its specific aspects was included. Only a small portion was devoted to what could be called general educational theory. The discussion of school procedures was given dogmatically with little consideration of the general theory on which it was based. Hall believed the teacher should realize education was necessary for civic responsibility, for individual material success, and for pious living which was necessary preparation for the world to come. He was convinced that popular education was essential to the maintenance of liberty and democratic institutions. "It *should be known* by all, that the best institutions of our country can be perpetuated no longer than intelligence and virtue continue among the common people. We may as well expect liberty in Turkey, as in these United States, when the common people cease to be enlightened. We may as well expect virtue in a band of robbers, as among our citizens, when ignorance is the characteristic of the common people." [32:17] He argued the need of education for moral character. "Many, it is to be feared, have no proper sense of the moral obligation resting upon them, in relation to teaching their children what is most important for them to know. If we are to judge from the conduct of many, we should conclude they had never seen that requisition in the word of God, 'Train up a child in the way he should go,' or that the apostolic injunction, 'Bring up your children in the nurture and admonition of the Lord,' had never fallen upon their ears . . . multitudes of parents seem to realize very little of the moral obligation that rests upon them, or, of their accountability to God! . . . That man who regards it as a matter of indifference, whether his children can read the sacred Scriptures understandingly or not . . . must be considered as not realizing his own moral accountability." [32:18] He scored the current "indifference to the importance, character, and usefulness of common schools" and pointed to the lack of preparation and inadequate compensation of teachers. After describing certain desirable character traits of the teacher, he devoted several chapters to "Practical Directions to Teachers." These chapters, two on "Government of the School" and one on "General Management of a School," are very similar to modern courses in "elementary school management," "rural school administration," or courses of similar nature. Teachers were advised how to control the school, urged to show no anger or partiality, to use common sense, kindness and firmness in governing, and to make every effort to keep the room quiet. Among the topics discussed are the use of threats, rewards, punishment, the personal habits of the teacher, the influence of the teacher, community relationships. The remainder of the book in which "the mode of teaching" spelling, reading, history, etc., is described bears some resemblance to present courses in "special methods of teaching the common branches."

A word should be said about the great vogue enjoyed by the book. Such was the need for a book of this kind that every copy of the first edition was sold within two weeks and the second edition almost as quickly. The New York legislature ordered 10,000 copies for its teachers; educational authorities in Kentucky urged every teacher to read it. [94:316] For nearly a quarter of a century it was the most popular textbook for teachers in the United States.

Jacob Abbott's essay *The Teacher* is similar to Hall's book in that it is concerned chiefly with practical suggestions for teaching. Like Hall he believed the teacher should realize that schooling was a valuable asset for individual success. Quaintly he commented on the practical importance of the mastery of the three R's. "Teaching a pupil to read, before he enters on the active business of life, is like giving a settler an axe, as he goes to seek his new home in the forest . . . but the art of ready reckoning is the plough, which will remain by him for years, and help him draw out from the soil an annual treasure. . . . The great object of the common schools in this country is, to teach the whole population to read, to write and to calculate. . . . The true policy is, to aim at making all good readers, writers and calculators; and to consider the duties of the school important, chiefly as practice in turning these arts to useful account." [1:638-39] Education, besides being essential to mundane success and the maintenance of democratic institutions, was also the way to salvation. The inculcation of piety was an important aim of education. "It has been my constant effort and one of the greatest sources of my enjoyment, to try to win my pupils to piety, and to create such an atmosphere in the school that conscience and moral principle and affection for the unseen Jehovah, should reign here." [1:668]

The outstanding book of this period and the book most responsible for emphasizing the professional course and the consideration of general theory was Page's *Theory and Practice of Teaching*. Not only does it reflect clearly the educational ideals of the period and the empirical, common-sense bases of classroom procedures then current, but it also shows the tendencies from which emerged the educational practice of later periods. Indeed, some of Page's conceptions of the educative process have a decidedly modern ring. For popularity this book ranks foremost. First published in 1847 it went through twenty-five editions by 1860. [94:328]

In essential outlook Page's book is integral with the educative literature of the period, but his conception of the needs of the teacher goes beyond that of Hall and Abbott. To him "truth is eternal and unchangeable." Piety is a prominent educational value. Almost every page reflects a deep religious fervor of which the following paragraph is typical: "We live in a Christian land. It is our glory, if not our boast that we have descended from an ancestry that feared God and reverenced his word. Very justly we attribute our superiority as a people over those who dwell in the darker portions of the world, to our purer faith derived from that precious fountain of truth—the Bible." [49:50]

Teachers are enjoined not to develop in their pupils a skeptical attitude. "At any rate, the teacher should be careful that his teaching and his example do not prejudice the youthful mind against these truths. It is a hazardous thing for a man to be skeptical by himself, even when he locks his opinions up in the secrecy of his own bosom; how great then is the responsibility of teaching the young to look lightly upon the only book that holds out to us the faith of immortality, and opens to us the hope of heaven!" [49:52]

Like its predecessor *Lectures on School Keeping*, Page's work has an omnibus character. Among the topics discussed one finds personal habits of teachers, their relations with the community, school government, care of schoolhouse, and attitudes toward children.

But as has already been pointed out, Page was also a vigorous apostle for a new and better pedagogy, and it was these new ideas which required more consideration of theory than was to be found in the Hall and Abbott books. Though he never mentioned Pestalozzi, the latter's influence is clearly discernible. He condemned the brutal punishment so prevalent at the time, though he did not thereby repudiate all use of corporal punishment. The teacher should realize that the rod should upon occasion be used, but never in anger. With Pestalozzi he abhorred the "pouring in process" and "passivity" conception of learning, devoting a whole section to pointing out the evils of this conception of education. Teachers should not force open the "mental gullets" of their pupils and "pour in," without mercy and without discretion whatever sweet thing they may have at hand even though they surfeit and nauseate the poor sufferer. The mind, by this process, becomes a mere *passive recipient*, taking in without much resistance whatever is presented till it is full. A passive recipient, he said, "is a two-gallon jug" but that is not the way to conceive the mind of a child. [49:89-90]

In yet another respect Page shows the influence of Pestalozzi, his insistence on the education of "the whole man—the body, the mind, and the heart." Pestalozzi spoke of "harmonious development." It should be noted that Page anticipated Spencer who defined education as preparation for complete living and L. P. Jacks who also thinks in terms of the education of the whole. The modernity of Page's theory is best illustrated by his emphasis on "curiosity" and "interests" as the bases of children's learning.

Thus Page in his greater emphasis on a professional curriculum anticipated the type of course later to follow. Beginning with weekly lectures of pedagogical advice in the first normal school, the course developed under Page a more professional content and tended to give some attention to general theory of education.

SECTION II

THE DEVELOPMENT OF NORMAL SCHOOLS AND THE TEACHING OF GENERAL EDUCATIONAL THEORY TO 1880

The slow growth of the normal schools was given a pronounced impetus, and professional education for teachers a new importance when the stimulating Oswego movement entered the scene about 1861.[4] Born during the Civil War period it apparently had little connection with that holocaust. It dominated American education until about 1880, when other movements from abroad brought in new emphases. Providing as it did a simple and readily applicable method of teaching the fundamental skills and knowledges, it fitted in well with a practical America, intent on exploiting a rich and virgin continent. The fact that this method of teaching was definite and supposedly very practical, that it was not difficult to learn, and that Edward A. Sheldon, initiator of the plan, was very aggressive in the educational field accounts in part for its rapid growth in popularity, essentially making it America's first great educational fad.

The Oswego plan takes its name from the Oswego Normal School,

---

[4] Up to 1861 only twelve normal schools had been established in the United States. This slow growth was due in part to the low regard in which the teaching profession was held. Rarely thought of as anything but a stepping stone to other more lucrative vocations, teaching frequently retained in the profession only those who suffered some physical deficiency or were otherwise handicapped in the struggle for a livelihood. [103:413-15]

whére Mr. Sheldon was principal. It was an imitation of an imperfect application of Pestalozzian methods. The Rev. Charles Mayo and his sister Elizabeth of England had visited Pestalozzi at Yverdon. Subsequently they had endeavored to put his principles into practice. All they succeeded in doing, however, was to capture the outer mechanical aspects of Pestalozzian pedagogy. It was an exhibit of the work of the Mayos in Toronto that gave the impetus to Sheldon's innovations. What impressed him most was the use made of objects for teaching. It is doubtful if he really understood Pestalozzi's theory, but so vigorously did he exploit the technique of "object teaching" that educators all over the country were attracted to this second-hand Pestalozzianism. [103:259-60, 80: I-II] No doubt the efforts of earlier admirers of Pestalozzi served to pave the way for the spread of this movement.[5]

The introduction and the rapid spread of the object teaching method had a momentous effect on the development of professional training of teachers. The number of normal schools rapidly multiplied. Mastery of the technique of object teaching came to be considered essential to the equipment of a teacher. New schools sprang up to supply this requisite training. In 1860 the number of normal schools was twelve; by 1868 there were thirty. [120:653] The initiation of the new method led not only to the establishment of new normal schools but also to the enrichment of teacher-training curricula. The "object teaching" plan, based as it was on Pestalozzi's philosophy, created a need for the study of his philosophy and stimulated interest in the history of education. Besides methods of giving object lessons, students at Oswego Normal School studied the principles of Pestalozzian pedagogy. The weekly lecture on "school keeping" was no longer considered adequate professional training. The teacher's course expanded to include methods courses, "art and science of teaching," history of education, mental philosophy, school economy, and other courses of a similar nature. A survey of normal schools conducted by Henry Barnard in 1867 reveals twenty-one different titles of professional courses. [120:651-826] It is not to be understood, however, that these were twenty-one different courses, for obviously the same content must frequently have been presented under different course titles.[6]

[5] Mention should be made of Hermann Krüse, Jr., a European student of Pestalozzian methods, who joined Sheldon in 1862 and remained twenty-five years. More than anyone at Oswego, Krüse understood Pestalozzi's philosophy.

[6] For example, "art and science of teaching" and "art of teaching" are mentioned as separate courses.

In this expanded teacher-training curriculum general educational theory began to find a place. The extent to which it had come into the professional courses is partly indicated by the titles used for these new courses. In a circular of the Oswego State Normal School appearing in 1870 "philosophy of education" was listed as a required course in the four-year classical curriculum. [80:64-7] The course "philosophy and history of education" was required in the two-year elementary curriculum. Of the twenty-one titles of professional courses of American teacher-training institutions, listed in Barnard's report mentioned above, nine seem to have included treatment of general theory in greater or less degree. These courses and the frequency with which they appear are herewith given. [95:51]

Title of Course	Frequency
Art and science of teaching	1
Art of teaching	1
History of education	5
Philosophy of instruction	2
Principles and methods of instruction (teaching)	2
Principles of education	2
School economy or management	5
Science of education (or teaching)	2
Theory and practice of teaching	14

Courses bearing titles which suggest educational theory appear in a report of a committee of the American Normal School Association appointed in 1869 to prepare a model course of study for normal schools. [156:294-95] In recommending a list of subjects for a two-year curriculum they included "theory and practice of teaching" to be taken throughout the two years, the content of which varied from semester to semester. In the second semester of the last year appeared "philosophy of education, including mental philosophy."

From these course titles found in normal-school curricula, one should not, however, conclude that general educational theory occupied a well-defined place in teacher training. An attempt to determine the actual place of general educational theory was made by scrutinizing the syllabi accompanying a report of the Committee of the American Normal School Association, by examining the curriculum at Oswego (which may be regarded as fairly typical of the normal schools of the time), and by examining the textbooks used in professional courses.

An examination of the syllabi accompanying the projected curriculum recommended by the committee of the American Normal School Association was made on the assumption that probably this group represented the best and most forward-looking practice of the day. The examination showed that general educational theory was not to occupy as large a place as the titles of courses might suggest, for the syllabi indicate that major emphasis was to be given the techniques of teaching and faculty psychology. However, in the course "theory and practice of teaching," scheduled for the second semester of the last year, the topics "discipline and management" and "history of education" were mentioned, which indicates that some study of general theory was intended. The syllabus as it bears upon "philosophy of education" is quoted in full. "Nervous mechanism; the senses, sensation, perception, observation, memory, reason, imagination, etc.; principles and methods of training inferred from above." This phrase, "principles and methods of training inferred from above," suggests some study of general educational theory.

Dearborn's study was examined for a description of the theory courses at Oswego. He says: "The theory courses such as mental and moral philosophy or philosophy of education, were a mixture of the history of education, physiological psychology, and general principles of education . . . the psychology was limited, and comprised discussions concerning the nature and order of development of the various 'faculties' of the child—mental, moral and physical —to which reference has already been made." [80:60] Dearborn then states some of the conceptions "which formed the framework of these theoretical or philosophical courses:

1. Begin with the senses.
2. Never tell a child what he can discover for himself.
3. Activity is a law of childhood. Train the child not merely to listen, but to do. Educate the hand.
4. Love of variety is a law of childhood—change is rest.
5. Cultivate the faculties in their natural order. First form the mind, then furnish it.
6. Reduce every subject to its elements, and present one difficulty at a time.
7. Proceed step by step. Be thorough. The measure of information is not what you can give, but what the child can receive.
8. Let every lesson have a definite point.
9. First develop the idea and then give the term. Cultivate language.
10. Proceed from the simple to the difficult, i.e., from the known to the

unknown, from the particular to the general, from the concrete to the abstract.

11. Synthesis before analysis—not the order of the subject, but the order of nature." [80:69]

The Pestalozzian pedagogy, based as it was on a definite philosophy of life, necessarily involved some philosophical study by the teachers of that day. Such topics as fitting instruction to the nature of the child, the principle of self-activity, and harmonious development are properly philosophical in nature. It is thus seen that general educational theory at least had a beginning at Oswego. Although the chief concern of the movement was with methods of teaching object lessons, it also brought about an effort to study some of the broad problems of education.

As for textbooks used in professional courses, those by Hall and Page, described in Section I, continued their popularity. Some of the new books which appeared during this period were examined in this study. The titles, listed here in full, throw some light on the emphases being made at that time. They reflect in a measure the educational climate of the period. One notices, for example, the use of the words "philosophy" and "principles." *American Education: Its Principles and Elements* by E. D. Mansfield (1850); *The Normal, or Methods of Teaching the Common Branches* by Alfred Holbrook (1859); *Science of Education, or the Philosophy of Human Culture* by John Ogden (1859); *A Manual of Elementary Instruction for the Use of Public and Normal Schools* by E. A. Sheldon[7] (1862); *School Economy: A Treatise on the Preparation, Organization, Employments, Government, and Authorities of Schools* by J. P. Wickersham (1864); *First Principles of Popular Education and Public Instruction* by S. S. Randall (1868); *In the School-Room, Chapters in the Philosophy of Education* by J. S. Hart (1868); *Normal Methods of Teaching* by Edward Brooks (1879).

These books were not nearly as broadly theoretical as their titles might suggest. "Philosophy of education" as understood by the authors seemed to include everything that had anything to do with education. "Philosophy" at this time was a very comprehensive term, including the natural sciences as well as what today would be understood as philosophy.[8] Philosophy and science were in fact used

[7] Essentially a book on the methods of object teaching, it was included to discover the rôle played by general theory in the technique of this system.

[8] The physical sciences all came under the title "natural philosophy"; psychology was called "intellectual philosophy"; general philosophy, "moral philosophy."

interchangeably. Thus the phrase "philosophy of education" was used for treatises which might more properly have borne such titles as "science of education" or "psychology of education."[9] Whether "philosophy," "principles," "science," or some other word was used in the title, the following topics were usually treated: psychology (faculty), importance of public education, school management, personal relationships of the teacher, pupil-teacher relationships, general teaching techniques, methods of teaching the school subjects. Approximately 80 per cent of the material in these books was concerned with topics of essentially a non-philosophical nature.

Again, it is not the intention here to present a complete report of the educational philosophy of the period, but rather to point to those factors within it which most directly throw light on the problem with which we are dealing. The examination of these books was undertaken with the belief that the nature and motives operative in the teaching of general educational theory of those times would best be seen in the broader conceptions which were advanced through writing and teaching. They reveal at one and the same time the prevailing philosophies and the corresponding sense of the needs of the teacher.

In society at that time Newtonian physics had established the belief that the universe and everything in the universe was governed by law. It was the task of science to discover these laws so they could be used to control the environment for man's welfare. Science meant the organization of phenomena in terms of certain abstract principles which seemed plausible and, seen uncritically, appeared to be borne out by phenomena. Laws were not specific, quantitative, dynamic relations observable in the realm of fluxing experience; they were rather immutable principles.

This notion was applied to education as well as to other specialized fields of endeavor. More and more the "common sense" and empirical advice such as were found in the Hall and Page books were displaced by broad general principles and organized into a "science of education." Science as seen by the writers mentioned above was a dialectical search for immutable laws that could be stated in static concepts which, when understood, would give fool-proof general directions for educational procedure. Ogden said his purpose was "so to present the whole subject of Human Culture and so to lay

---

[9] "The phrase 'philosophy of education' was used in about the same way that science of education was used." Noble, S. G., "Beginnings of a Science of Education." [139]

open and enforce the principles of right Education and Teaching, that the humblest may understand." [48:iv] "The Science of Education," he said, "is based upon immutable principles. . . . They exist in the very nature of things, and are co-extensive with man's existence." [48:ix] Wickersham said his work "professes to be a practical treatise based on scientific principles. . . . Teaching is more an art than a science; but it is art based either upon observation of facts or the apprehension of principles." [67:vii] Similarly, Brooks wrote, "Teaching is a Science and an Art. It embraces a system of truths that admit of scientific statement and may be woven together with the thread of philosophical principles." [48:iii] Mansfield stated his book was philosophical in nature and his purpose "to aid in contemplating those higher and nobler principles which lie beyond the details of books and the modes of instruction; in fine, those principles which concern universal nature and direct the destiny of the soul." [46:vii]

In a footnote, Mansfield made a very interesting observation about the value of philosophy: "Some say this generalizing, *philosophizing* is of no use; we want to learn *practical* every-day things. Now it is precisely because general elementary *principles* are of the *greatest use*, the most practical of all things, that they should be learned. . . . So, many of the rules of human life, as those in the Book of Proverbs, are general principles, which, if adhered to, will make men wise and great. In fact, *generalization* is the only means by which we can acquire or retain the constant accumulations of knowledge from age to age." [46:34]

The widespread acceptance of the concepts of faculty psychology afforded a second reason for the rise in importance of general theory. This faculty psychology, as is well known, was the theoretical basis of Pestalozzi's methods. There was a growing belief that an understanding of this psychology and of the educational principles based on it was essential for good teaching. The note was sounded that the teacher must understand the nature of the child especially as learner, and proceed "according to nature." It was held that the teacher must "understand his materials even as agriculturists and artists must understand their materials." [48:15] "The entire soul in all its faculties, which need education, and not any one of its talents," [46:vii] should be considered. "Education must be adapted to philosophic 'laws of childhood,'" wrote Sheldon. His extremely detailed treatment of school procedure was prefaced by an essay emphasizing the need for understanding children in the light of "faculty psychology." [57:13-4] So important was this notion of "faculties" that education was often defined as the "harmonious development of the faculties."

"What is the ultimate object [of education]?" Mansfield asked. "No less than to develop all the faculties of the human soul to the utmost extent of which they are susceptible." [45:55]

Randall stated: "The true philosophy of education is therefore to be sought in a careful investigation of our mental and moral faculties. . . . Man is an immortal being, endowed by his Creator with all those faculties, as well of mind as of body, which, properly appreciated and faithfully used, were designed to contribute, in the highest possible degree, to his happiness and well-being here and hereafter." [54:10]

The belief that teachers must understand the aims of education was a further reason in the minds of these educators for the importance of educational philosophy. "All of these objects (aims)," Wickersham said, "must be considered in arranging a course of study. . . . With these objects in view, the teacher must select such studies . . . as will be best calculated to promote them." [67:71-2] Hart devoted an entire chapter to "What is Education?" and answered, "Education is developing, in due order and proportion, whatever is good and desirable in human nature." [34:XXX] Likewise Randall wrote a chapter, "Objects, Means and Ends of Education," in which he says: "In all our efforts to improve and perfect our systems of Public Instruction, it is of paramount importance clearly to understand and constantly to keep in view the objects, aims and ends of Education." [54:227] According to Ogden, God has a Purpose in the world and the teacher must discover this purpose and plan his work accordingly. [48:174-75]

Another reason why these writers thought general educational theory important was their belief that education should affect many aspects of life and that teachers should have a broad point of view. They wished to develop in the teachers the broad point of view which they themselves had supposedly achieved. This attitude must have been due in part to the concept generally held at the time and undoubtedly of Pestalozzian origin that education was the harmonious development of all the faculties. Teachers thus "harmoniously developed" were more capable of producing a like result in the children. The educational leaders of the period were interested not only in the all-round development of the individual as a person, but in him also as a member of society.

This effort to develop a broad point of view and ability to see relationships is revealed in the sub-title of Ogden's book, *The Philosophy of Human Culture.* The subject matter does not belie the sub-title. He attempted to show how religion, the physical sciences, the arts, mathematics, languages, metaphysics all contribute to intellectual development and how they relate to education and to each other. The assumption was that accumulation of knowledge in many fields would in and by itself lead to a crystallization of a broad and comprehensive view of life. In his two chapters, "Errors of the Cave" and "Men of One Idea," Hart urged teachers to acquire knowledge in many fields. "The workman who is to operate upon a substance (youth) so subtle and so varying must not be a man of *one idea*—who knows one thing and nothing more. . . . Hence the necessity on the part of those who would excel in the profession of teachers, of endeavoring continually to enlarge the bounds of their knowledge. Hence the error of those who think that to teach anything well it is necessary to know only that one thing. . . . Every teacher needs a cultivated taste, a disciplined outlook, and that enlargement of views which results only from enlarged knowledge." [34:79-80]

The changing conception of school control furnished another reason for the consideration of educational theory. Force in the schoolroom was being displaced with moral suasion. Teachers were urged to love their pupils and rule through kindness. This radical departure (in theory if not in practice) from the brutal discipline that characterized the American school of this and earlier periods necessitated considerable discussion of the merits of the new theory and methods of administering it. Obedience and subordination were required but were not to be forced except as a last resort. Teachers should lead the children rather than force them.

In a chapter on "Loving the Children," Hart said, *"You must love the children.* You must love each particular child. You must become interested in each child, not for what it is to you or to the class, but for what it is in itself, as a precious jewel, to be loved and admired, for those immortal qualities and capacities which belong to it as a human being." [34:96]

This was not to say that kindness should diminish the place of authority. Children were to learn to respect authority whether it came from God, the parent, the teacher, or the state. Hart said in a later chapter: "Obedience is doing a thing because another, having competent authority, has enjoined it. The motive necessary to constitute any act an act of obedience, is a reference to a will and authority of another. The child receives as true what his parents say, and because they say it. . . . I must learn to obey my father, simply because he is my father, and because as such he has the right to command me, if thereby I am to learn, for a like reason to obey my heavenly Father. . . . Obedience is yielded to authority, and authority is based on right and power. . . . This sense of subordination and obedience to appointed and rightful authority is of the very essence of civil government." [34 : 105-10]

Another reason for interest in theoretical matters was found in the Christian philosophy which dominated the thinking of this period. Central in this philosophy was the belief that life on earth was a transitional state whose chief value lay in preparation for a future existence. To this end each of these books was permeated with a deep religious feeling; Biblical allusions and references to the Deity were found on almost every page. The authors wished so to imbue the prospective teachers with Christian ideals and virtues that they siezed every opportunity to reaffirm them. Emphasis was placed on the importance of the teacher passing on to the children these ideals —an obligation owed to the children and to God.

Randall thus urged the importance of religious instruction : "The great truths that we are immortal and responsible beings—that the will of our Creator, in reference to our conduct and our duty, in thought no less than in word and deed, throughout every period of our intelligent existence, has been communicated to us—and that our present and future well-being, in time and throughout eternity, are wholly and inevitably dependent upon the affections we now hourly and daily cultivate. . . . These convictions, based upon the paramount authority of Divine Revelation, must constitute the corner-stone of every sound and enlightened system of Christian education." [54 : 13-4]

Hart said, "This then is the first principle that governs us in the work here assigned us. The fear of God is the beginning of knowledge. We who are teachers endeavor to show that we ourselves fear God, and we inculcate the fear of Him as the first and highest duty of our scholars." [34 : 202]

In the Christian philosophy, faith was fundamental and teachers were admonished not to arouse any skepticism. "Another faculty that shoots up into full growth in the very morning and springtime of life, is Faith. I speak . . . of that faculty of the human mind which leads a child to believe instinctively what is told him.

. . . How slow and tedious would be the first steps in knowledge, were the child born, as some teachers seem trying to make him, a skeptic, that is, with a mind which refuses to receive anything as true, except what it has first proved by experience and reason! . . . How cruel to force the confiding young heart into premature skepticism, by compelling him to hunt up reasons for everything, when he has reasons, to him all sufficient, in the fact that father, mother, or teacher told him so." [34:34-5]

Even science was not to be allowed to disturb religious faith. Wickersham disposed of the problem, science versus religion, as follows: ". . . but to the believer in the perfections of God, no antagonism between science and religion is possible. God does not contradict himself. The Truth in His Works cannot invalidate in the least particular the truth of His Word. . . . All true education is religious. Systems of science are but the thoughts of God. . . . All science, therefore, leads to God. Its laws all converge and unite in Him; and the student cannot reach his journey's end until he rests safe on the Savior's bosom." [67:368]

Rooted in this Christian philosophy was the generally accepted theological dogma of total depravity of man. This carried the practical application of the need for "discipline." This conception of the nature of the individual meant that the evil nature of the child should be subdued, that his will should be subjected to the will of his elders, parents, and teachers. As mentioned above, the harshness and brutality that prevailed both at home and at school were being tempered by the humanizing trend of the times which softened to some extent the force of the theological conception of depravity as applied to education. Yet in practice that conception virtually remained in effect. Through a program of rigorous control at home and at school, the child was developed into an individual who would readily accede to established custom. Docility and conformity were highly prized.

Ogden wrote: "But we have unbounded faith in the efficacy of the remedial agents, provided by the merciful Being who first gave us our powers, and commanded us to keep and perpetuate them. But since man failed to do this, through a greater than creative kindness, the same Being has provided a ransom in the atonement, so ample as to reach to the lowest depths of his depravity, renovating his moral nature, healing his moral disease, and thereby rendering it possible, at least, by a course of education and discipline, by obedience to the laws of his being, and a strict observance of the laws of God to retract those steps, and regain, if not a primitive and absolute state of perfection, at least, to attain to the sublimest heights of human excellence." [48:12]

According to Wickersham, discipline was one of four chief aims. *"Discipline is an End of Study.*—The human body in infancy is weak, it needs to be invigorated and toughened; the human intellect is feeble, it needs to be developed and strengthened; the human passions are wild and rash, they need to be restrained and guided; the human will is fitful and perverse, it needs to be trained to docility and educated to husband and direct its power. This invigorating and toughening of the body, . . . restraining and guiding the passions, training and educating the will, is discipline; and it is one of the highest aims of study to secure it." [67:121]

In the minds of the writers of this period Christian righteousness and faith as an educational ideal embraced the ideal of good citizenship. Consequently teachers must understand and appreciate the ideals of democracy and pass on to their pupils a like understanding and appreciation. The civic value of education was emphasized in the literature under consideration. Educated, God-fearing, God-loving Christians made the best citizens. Mansfield stated: "American education, in order to attain the perfection of society and perpetuate the institutions of freedom must adapt itself . . . to whatever is peculiar in America, peculiar in Christian civilization. . . . The idea of American education, then, is of an education, in fact and theory, in conformity with the idea of a complete republic; in conformity with the idea of a Christian republic." The foundations of knowledge, he said, were: "1. The idea of its government, contained in the Constitution. 2. The idea of modern science, developed in modern civilization. 3. The idea of Christianity, developed in the Bible." [46:59-60]

Teachers must understand that education developed economic independence, tended to prevent crime, and helped to make sure of the safety of property. "Schools, then, especially schools in which moral and religious truth is inculcated, are the most powerful means of lessening crime, and of lessening the costly and frightful apparatus of criminal administration. As schoolhouses and churches increase in the land, jails and prisons diminish. As knowledge is diffused, property becomes secure and rises in value. A community, therefore, is bound to see that its members are properly educated, if for no other reason, in mere self-defense. The many must be educated in order that the many may be protected." [34:258]

There were other beliefs about education and the nature of the individual that come within the category of general theory, such as the belief that all knowledge was derived from sense-impressions, that education should be conducted on the plane of reason rather than on the level of rote memorization, and that the teacher should seek to elicit "self-activity and self-expression." These notions came into vogue largely through the influence of the Oswego movement which paraded under the flag of Pestalozzianism. Perhaps the notion of sense-empiricism came close to being applied in the object-teaching method. The theoretical discussions and actual school practices of the day do not indicate that the other notions had specific connotations. None the less, it is important to note that the theorists of the day at least thought that they were directing educational efforts along the lines of these new ideas.

No effort has been made to report all of the conceptions current at the time. Enough has been said to make it clear that although professional courses were chiefly concerned with faculty psychology and methods of managing the school and teaching the school subjects, some attention was given to the consideration of broader theoretical problems. The need for greater emphasis on the theory of education than has hitherto obtained was due to the prevailing beliefs about child nature, the nature of learning, the ends most worth striving for.

It should be added, however, that in view of the extreme immaturity of most of the students (few having more than an elementary education), and the ponderous and involved style of most of the writers, much of this philosophical material must have been meaningless. The discussions were frequently so abstract that it is difficult to see how they could have had much functional value.

Some attention was also directed in the study to the texts used in the study of history of education which developed into a separate course during this period. Three books were examined: *Education: History of Education, Ancient and Modern, and A Plan of Culture and Instruction* by H. I. Smith (1842); *History and Progress of Education from the Earliest Times to the Present* by Philobiblius (pseud.) (1859); *Twelve Lectures on the History of Pedagogy* by W. N. Hailman (1874).

It does not seem probable that the first two books were of great value in broadening the viewpoints of the students. Exceedingly factual in content, they attempted to relate the history of education of all peoples from the beginning of recorded history. They also attempted to describe the educational systems in force during the period, thus including some of the material now treated in comparative education courses. The effort to cover so much ground about matters of which the authors had only a passing knowledge resulted in an extremely sketchy and meager discussion of really important material. Smith, for example, devoted barely two pages to Rousseau; Philobiblius, one-fourth of a page. The summary treatment of Rousseau was due to the religious bias of the writers. Crowded into the same cover with Smith's *History* was also his *Plan of Culture and Instruction*, similar in content to the material found in the Page and Hall books.

Hailman's *Lectures on Pedagogy*, which came out twenty-nine years after Smith's book, was much the most valuable of the three texts. In it is reflected the philosophical movement which reached its height in the eighties and nineties. It was less prejudiced, and relatively more space was devoted to the philosophical aspects of educational history. Although academic in nature, it probably was more helpful in expanding the viewpoints of the students than the other two books, and thus came closer to the purpose of general educational theory.

In summary it may be said the Oswego movement, while it gave vogue to some of Pestalozzi's educational theories, tended ultimately to place greatest emphasis upon specific teaching procedures. Mastery of the techniques of object teaching rather than thorough grasp of the philosophy upon which it was based became the chief concern of teachers. [103 : 437-41]

Several professional courses began to emerge from the one professional course, "lectures on school-keeping," or "theory and art of teaching," the most distinct of which were the courses in methods, school economy, and history of education. General educational theory, while not confined to any one course, came to occupy an ever larger place in courses with such titles as philosophy of instruction or education, art or science of education, and history of education.

Although critical of some of the educational practices of the day, general educational theory as found in the textbooks was essentially a *status quo* philosophy in that the current assumptions underlying the economic system, the government, and Christian theology were not questioned. These writers were chiefly concerned, as were the earlier writers, with perpetuating and rationalizing the then generally accepted patterns of democratic, utilitarian, Christian America. If only these standards could be translated into human conduct, it was believed maximum happiness would be assured in the present life and in the life to come.

The Oswego movement became so highly formalized and fell so far short of realizing the hopes of its devotees that the 1880's found educational vitality at a low point. The time seemed ripe for an educational renaissance.

SECTION III

THE TEACHING OF GENERAL EDUCATIONAL THEORY
FROM 1880 TO 1905

Economically America experienced during the period from 1880 to 1905 the greatest material progress hitherto made by any people. With unlimited natural resources, with an abundance of efficient labor being imported from Europe in shiploads, with the ever-increasing number of inventions, the wealth of the country doubled and trebled. During this period some of the great fortunes of the nation—the Gould, Vanderbilt, Harriman, Rockefeller, Carnegie fortunes—were being made; even the depressions of 1873 and 1893 were but temporary setbacks. The frontier allowed plenty of room for expansion, served as a safety valve in times of economic stress, and a place for American workmen to turn to when dissatisfied with conditions in the Industrial East. The building of railroads and factories and consequent growth of cities, the opening of the cattle, mining, fishing, and lumbering industries in the West, the industrialization of the South, the expansion of agriculture through the Homestead Act and the invention of labor-saving machinery, the acquiring of new territories in the Pacific—these things commanded the genius of the American people. [72:XIX, 85: sec. 3, 4]

This great expansion of industry and agriculture was accompanied by expansion in education. Elementary and especially secondary and higher institutions of learning rapidly increased in number and in student enrollment. Throughout the Middle and Far West state universities, land-grant colleges, and great numbers of denominational liberal arts colleges were established. The larger enrollments produced an expansion of college curricula to new and diversified areas.

This growth was shared by teacher-training institutions. By 1900 there were 170 public normal schools and 118 private normal schools. [94:329] To meet the ever-growing demand for high school teachers the "Normal Departments," previously established as external attachments at some of the Western universities,[10] gradually were incorporated as integral parts of the institutions under "chairs of pedagogy" or departments of education. These officially recognized departments of education were established first at the University of Michigan in 1879, at the University of Wisconsin in 1885, at Indiana University and Cornell University in 1886.[11] Such rapid increase in the number of publicly supported normal schools and the rise of departments of education at the state universities reflect not only the material expansion of this period, but also the increased realization of the importance of professional education for teachers. As will be later shown, the larger place given to teacher training in the educational setup was shared by those courses dealing with educational theory.

By 1880 the force of the Oswego movement had spent itself; even interest in professional teacher education had slackened.[12] But while this movement was on the wane, other forces gathered strength. Influences from abroad were already at work which were to inject new life into the normal school idea and into education generally. By 1873 the Frøbelian doctrines of child activity and creative self-expression preached for two decades by German emigrés establishing kindergartens throughout the country had become widespread and reached the proportions of a movement. [103:XXI] During the 70's and 80's, through an emphasis on a practical education in which the natural sciences were considered of most worth, Herbert Spencer and Thomas H. Huxley, by lectures in this country and by stimulating books, [61, 62, 39] challenged the educational thinking of the time. Francis W. Parker, who had studied abroad, in his work at Quincy (Massachusetts) and at the Cook County Normal

[10] Indiana University established a "normal seminary" in 1852; Iowa University, a normal department in 1855; and the University of Wisconsin in 1863. As "their work was decidedly elementary in character, consisting mainly in reviews of the common school subjects, plus a few lectures on the art of teaching and in some cases observation and practice in a model school," the normal departments were held in very low regard by the rest of the university. [89:2]

[11] Although the first permanent chair of pedagogy was established at the University of Iowa in 1873, it was shared with the chair of general philosophy. [11:145]

[12] The United States Commissioner of Education said in his Report for 1888-1889 that the year 1870 marked the beginning of an "educational renaissance." For this he gave two reasons: "The kind of teacher training started by Peirce was 'giving out' and increased educational activity in Europe, especially in Germany." [156:297]

Kruse, after sifting considerable source material, describes the period 1868-1890 as the period of "criticism and discontent. During the 70's the morale of the normal school was alarmingly low." [95:53]

School (Illinois) reiterated, revived, reinterpreted, and demonstrated the practicability of such Pestalozzian-Fröbelian ideas as child freedom and child activity. G. Stanley Hall, likewise a student of German universities, through his work at Johns Hopkins and later at Clark University and through his voluminous writing, generated interest in child nature and adolescence and in the adapting of school procedures to suit child nature. William T. Harris, as superintendent of schools at St. Louis and later as U. S. Commissioner of Education, championed the Hegelian philosophy with its theistic idealism, its implicit dualism, and its rigorous disciplinary program of external control. Later, in the 90's, Charles DeGarmo and Frank and Charles McMurry, as professors of education and as prolific writers of professional textbooks, advanced the Herbartian ideas of interest, apperception, correlation in opposition to the Hegelian position.

One may well comment on the fact that this educational activity had its origin in Europe. The reason for this importation was due not entirely to the fact that Europe, especially Germany, was the scene of much creative thinking in philosophy, psychology, and in education generally but also that America was absorbed in other fields of endeavor—the amassing of wealth, the subjugation of the continent, the invention of machines. America was content to borrow from the Old World in the non-exploitive fields.[13] In music, art, literature, architecture, the patterns were chiefly European. Likewise in philosophy of education no great amount of creative thinking was done. Thus it happened that the great educational movements which pulled American education in divers directions were not native to this country. Not until the arrival of James and Dewey did America evolve a native philosophy of education and of life.[14]

These forces from abroad, chiefly German, served to make this period from the standpoint of educational philosophy one of the most interesting in the history of American education. The result of this philosophic interest was to push the teaching of general educational theory into the largest relative place it had yet or has since occupied in the teacher-training curriculum.

[13] Civil service reform should also be mentioned as a problem which absorbed the time of some of the best minds in America. [85:97]

[14] Further evidence of "borrowing" in the field of teacher training is to be noted in the widespread use of European textbooks. English authors whose books were widely used were Tate, Fitch, Payne, Quick, and Laurie. Translations by American educators of Compayré, Perz, Radestock, and Rosenkranz were also popular.

Even before 1880 there was evidence that the more definitely theoretical course had emerged. This is shown by a study made by Ogden in 1874. Of the twenty-eight replies to the question, "What constitutes your professional course?" the following statements are quoted (the statements of more purely theoretical courses are italicized):

Answer 1. "Four weeks psychology, twelve ·weeks discussion of school organization and *principles of instruction. History of Education,* seven weeks, *Philosophy of Education* (Rosenkranz' *Pedagogics and Lectures*) 39 weeks. Practical teaching in model school—methods of teaching in connection with the common branches as above, 104 weeks."

Answer 11. "First year of course: 60 lectures on school management and *the art of teaching*; 60 days experimental teaching in the presence of teacher and classmates. Second year: Class teaching in Training School. Third year: 50 lectures, *philosophy of education,* school system and laws."

Answer 26. "First term: *Philosophy and history of education;* school economy; civil government and school law. Methods of giving object lessons and of teaching the subjects of the elementary course. . . ."

Answer 27. "*Philosophy of education* (Textbook, Tate's *Philosophy of Education* as a basis of recitation, lecture, and discussion.) Wickersham's *School Economy,* with lectures and discussions. School laws, school history, lectures." [48: 216-29]

These four answers show the differentiation of professional subject matter that has occurred by their references to such courses as history of education, methods of teaching, and school economy. They also show the existence of the more definitely theoretical course in the references to "philosophy of education" and to the use of Rosenkranz' *Pedagogics and Lectures* later published as *Philosophy of Education.* The fact that this book was used as a text marks this course as philosophical as we here use the term. According to Kilpatrick [90:61] this text was the first to give vogue to the course title "philosophy of education." An examination of its contents[15] shows the book to be highly philosophical and to come the nearest of all textbooks mentioned heretofore to the subject matter of general educational theory. This is not so true, however, of courses using Tate's *Philosophy of Education.* In spite of its title, it is more

---

[15] See pages 53 f. for discussion of this textbook.

concerned with psychology or mental philosophy, as it was then called.

The tendency to diversify professional curricula and to give a larger place to the more purely theoretical courses is further shown in a study made by Taylor in 1886. Answers from fifty representative schools to questions concerning curriculum offerings show considerable agreement on a few basic courses. "Two-thirds of these schools give methods, psychology and school economy as distinct branches of study, one-third name science (or philosophy of education)[16] and one-half name history of education." [151 : 398] It is significant that one-third of these schools mentioned science or philosophy of eduction and that one-half mentioned history of education, the more purely theoretical courses.

The "Chicago Committee" on Methods of Instruction and Courses of Study in Normal Schools reported in 1889 "a material gain in the attention given to the study of professional subjects." The time apportionments for the various courses as given by the thirty-five schools included in the Report are as follows: [143]

Number of Schools	Courses	Average Number of Weeks
33	History of education	13
27	Science of education (or philosophy of)*	$15\frac{2}{3}$
30	Methods in elementary branches	$31\frac{3}{4}$
33	Mental science (psychology)	$20\frac{1}{3}$
23	School economy	$14\frac{1}{3}$
3	Report the subject without division	

* Parentheses mine.

It is important here to notice the relatively large number of institutions which gave courses of a theoretical nature. Thirty-three out of the thirty-five schools that answered gave history of education for an average of thirteen weeks.[17] Twenty-seven gave science or philosophy of education for fifteen and two-thirds weeks. This last item is the more significant in view of the apparent effort to include psychology (faculty) under "mental science." It is not here concluded that these courses were all of a strictly theoretical

[16] Parentheses mine.

[17] This course, as taught at that time, was frequently a history of the development of educational theories and thus deserves to be mentioned in this connection. Luckey characterized one of the popular texts in history of education as "more appropriately, a history of the philosophy of education." [98 : 156] In 1906 Bolton said history of education "frequently means in some institutions the same as principles of education." [123]

nature, but even with all the allowances that must be made for the inaccurate nomenclature, one is justified in concluding that general educational theory was by 1889 occupying a relatively important place in the curriculum.

Moreover, it should be mentioned that courses in school economy and methods in elementary branches also included some treatment of broadly theoretical material. It has already been shown that Wickersham's *School Economy* contained material of this sort. Texts on methods of teaching usually contained one or more chapters on such subjects as aims of education, the function of the teacher or the school, and citizenship and moral education. For example, a text bearing the title *On the Province of Methods of Teaching* [36] was not so much a treatise on teaching technique as it was a collection of quotations from classic writers.

The fact that the course titles do not indicate clearly the nature of the subject matter dealt with makes it difficult to form conclusions on the listed offerings of institutions. Taylor in his report [151:400] alluded to the differences of opinion as to the content of the various courses, quoting the contradicting definitions of several schoolmen on the scope of "science of teaching" and "art of teaching." This great variety of titles in use in 1890 and the difficulty of accurate classification is shown in the following list prepared by Frazier [83:t4] from course titles of ten selected colleges and universities. Only those groups including courses likely to deal more directly with general educational theory are listed. Two groups omitted were concerned with methods courses and school economy.

Course Titles in Pedagogy in 10 Selected Colleges and Universities, in (or about) 1890

Group 1	*Group 2*
Educational psychology (2)*	Didactics (2)
Logic and psychology	Education in the United States
Mental science	Educational science and systems
Philosophy of education (2)	Libraries and schools
Psychology	Literature of education
Psychology and moral philosophy	Pedagogics
Pure psychology and ethics	Pedagogics; seminary
Theoretical and critical; principles, etc.	Practical; the arts of teaching and governing, etc.
Theory of teaching	Science of education
	Seminary; educational problems (2)
* Number of institutions.	The school (2)

Group 4

Comparative study of educational systems
Foreign school systems
History of education (4)
History of education; ancient and medieval
History of education; ancient and modern
History of education; modern
History of education and philosophy
History of educational theories and practice
(History and philosophy of education)
Seminary

The similarity of courses in Group 1 with several in Group 2, as suggested by the titles, and the variety of titles within each group indicate the confusion in the field and the arbitrary judgment which the classifier must use in tabulating them. With all its disadvantages, however, this list shows the variety in titles of the more purely theoretical courses. Of the ten colleges, two mention philosophy of education. Other course titles that indicate philosophical material are: logic and psychology, psychology and moral philosophy, pure psychology and ethics, theoretical and critical; principles, etc.; theory of teaching, educational science and systems, education in the United States, literature of education, pedagogics, science of education, and all the courses of Group 4.

The number of theoretical courses and their relative position in the curriculum from 1890 to 1900 are shown in a study of "pedagogical courses" made by Luckey [98:157][18] of twenty state universities among the first to establish departments of education. Only the figures for five-year periods are here quoted.

The courses most broadly philosophical are those in Group 1, History of education, School systems, and Educational classics; and in Group 2, Theory of education, Science of education, Philosophy of education, Institutes of education. The "practical" and "psychological" courses in Groups 3 and 4 are largely technical and scientific in character. In 1890-1891 seven universities gave, as shown by Groups 1 and 2, twelve courses of a more purely theoretical nature as against seven courses of a more technical nature, as shown by Groups 3 and 4. At this time it would seem educational leaders thought the most valuable professional training for pros-

[18] Luckey complained that the terms "philosophy of education," "science of education," "principles of education," "institutes of education," and "educational theory," although different in meaning yet as titles of university courses were used to cover almost the same ground.

PEDAGOGICAL

	GROUP 1				GROUP 2				
Department Represented	History of Education	School Systems	Educational Classics	Historical (Total)	Theory of Education	Science of Education	Philosophy of Education	Institutes of Education	Theoretical (Total)
1890 a Courses	7	5	2	..	7	1	2	2	..	5
1891 b Hours	..	18	6	..	24	4	3⅓	5⅓	..	14⅔
1895 a Courses	19	16	11	2	29	4	2	6	4	16
1896 b Hours	..	69	36	10	115	13	4	20	14	51
1899 a Courses	20	18	14	3	35	4	2	9	3	18
1900 b Hours	..	94	43	8	145	15	6	31	10	62

* Observation and practice teaching not included.

pective teachers was the study of history of education (largely a history of educational philosophies) and theory, science, or philosophy of education. Again, the reminder must be offered that these so-called theoretical courses dealt in greater or less degree with what today would be classified as psychology, for the demarcation between philosophy and psychology at that time was not clear. Even so, one psychology course as such was offered. This emphasis upon "historical" and "theoretical" courses as against the "practical" and "psychological" courses will later be shown to be due to (1) the greater academic respectability of history and philosophy on university campuses as compared with methods courses; (2) the interest in educational theories, past and present, which was stimulated by the various contending philosophies of the day; and (3) the then undeveloped state of psychology and accompanying courses in tests and measurements.

By 1895-1896 nineteen of the twenty institutions examined had established departments of education. There is a total of twenty-nine offerings of "historical" and sixteen "theoretical" courses, or a combined total of forty-five courses in Groups 1 and 2 as against forty-one, the combined total of the more technical. At this time it would seem the "historical" and "theoretical" courses were still considered the most valuable at the universities, but "practical" courses had evidently found considerable favor, for in five years they had jumped from six to twenty-nine. The increase in courses in "method of instruction" probably reflected the Herbartian peda-

COURSES

Group 3				Group 4			
Supervision and Management	Method of Instruction	Art of Teaching	Practical (Total)	Applied Psychology	Genetic Psychology	Child Study	Psychological (Total)
2	3	1	6	1	..	..	1
5	7	2	14	3⅓	..	..	3⅓
11	13	5	29*	7	..	5	12
33	32	11	76	26	..	14	40
14	13	4	31	11	3	12	26
44	44	10	98	43	8	31	82

gogy with its emphasis on "general method" or principles of teaching applicable to all the school subjects. The nature of the Herbartian pedagogy will be outlined later, when some of the books written to advance this movement are discussed.[19] The point should be made here, however, that courses in general method were themselves largely theoretical in that a study of the philosophy on which the methods were based formed a large part of the course.

By 1900 the course offerings in Groups 1 and 2, which are thought of as representing more nearly the philosophical interest, had grown to lesser relative positions in the curriculum, the total being fifty-three as against fifty-seven for Groups 3 and 4. However, the total number of hours scheduled for courses in Groups 1 and 2—207 hours—as against those scheduled for courses in Groups 3 and 4—180 hours—shows the more broadly philosophical courses still outweighing the more technical courses. It will be noticed that the course consistently maintaining a lead throughout was history of education. The increase of courses offered in the psychological group from twelve to twenty-six in five years' time indicates the growing importance of psychology with its greater dependence upon biology and scientific experimentation, and portends the division of professional education which was to see the greatest progress in the next quarter century.[20]

In preparing this table, Luckey found it difficult to classify under

[19] See pages 56-59.
[20] This important movement will be outlined in Section 4.

the more usual heads all the courses found in the catalogues. Of the additional courses mentioned the following suggest general educational theory: kindergarten and primary instruction, secondary education, educational doctrines, educational ideals, Herbartian pedagogy, leading present topics and problems of education, educational reforms, current educational movements, aesthetics in relation to education, sociology in relation to education, ethics, development of character, history of philosophy, elements of pedagogy.

To explain this high proportion of university courses devoted largely to general educational theory, it is necessary to review the founding of the chairs of pedagogy especially established to meet the demand for professional courses for secondary teachers. In many universities pedagogy was organized first as a subdivision under the department of philosophy. This was true of Harvard, Pennsylvania, Minnesota, Illinois, Iowa, California, and Chicago Universities. [89:9] Even when the chair of pedagogy was organized as an independent department, there was a tendency for it later to join with the philosophy department. At the University of Wisconsin in 1888 the chair of the "Art and Science of Teaching" was changed to the chair of "Philosophy and Pedagogy," the purpose being, according to the professor in charge, to "bring the study of education into closer relations with its cognate branches."[21] The same shift from a separate department to a subdepartment under philosophy occurred at Indiana and Ohio Universities. [89:10]

The emphasis on theoretical courses in universities was principally due to the belief that these departments or subdepartments of education should not offer the same type of work as that offered by the normal schools. The task of preparing teachers for the secondary schools was thought to be different in aim and in method from that of preparing elementary school teachers. In discussing the "Professorship of Pedagogics," Boone, a contemporary, wrote:

Somewhat different, in respect to both organization and aim is the university professorship of Pedagogics.

"The distinctive function of the university," says Rev. R. H. Quick, "is not action, but thought. And the best thing the university can do for schoolmasters is to employ some of their keenest intellects in considering education on the side of theory, and in teaching principles respecting it as have been or can be established."

Both the normal school and the professorship have like educational bearings. The former, however, is special; the latter general. [11 : 42]

The low regard in which the normal schools were held, especially the "normal departments" located at universities where the work was often below the level of preparatory work, created an urgent need for courses in education which would be considered academically respectable and worthy of study on the higher level. [89 : 10] The professors of pedagogy were compelled to raise their work above the normal schools with their "dependence upon devices and mechanical methodology," to gain any respect from their university colleagues. This opinion that the teaching of methods was the province of the normal schools, quite beneath the dignity of the university, tended to fix attention upon history and philosophy of education. Boone thus urged the teaching of these courses in 1889:

. . . and now, especially, the history of education and its institutions. This involves not only the education of the states, ancient and modern, but the accompanying social and political forms, custom and creed, antecedents and environment, and the physical and other conditions which determine the institutional life. It is a work, viewed from the pedagogical side, peculiarly within the province of the university.

. . . Philosophy of education is, then, a phase of general philosophy, rests upon its constituent knowledges, borrows its deductions and is conditioned by them. Theories of mind, and the individual responsibility; prevalent estimates of the social life and the functions of the State; the changed interpretations of natural phenomena and forces, all contribute to the shaping of educational doctrine and its ultimate creed. The enlargement of university pedagogy on the side indicated is one of the hopeful signs of the day.[22] [11 : 147-48]

The effort to make education courses at the university extremely academic and philosophical is shown by the following announcement of Professor Arnold Tompkins' program in the Catalogue of the University of Illinois for 1895-1896:

2. *The Aim or Motive in Teaching.* (a) The true, or universal aim, as determined by the nature of life. (b) The various aims as consciously or unconsciously held at present by different countries and classes of people. Such diversity accounted for and unified. (c) The aim as shown in variation through historical development—the study of historical ideals. Winter term.

[22] The consistently high place of history of education in the Luckey tables and its prominence in the university study of education is explained by the fact that more than any other course it "enjoyed the benign favor of the scrupulous academic gods." [129]

3. *The Universal Form of Method in Education,* as determined by the nature of life. (a) In its subjective aspect. (b) In its objective aspect. (c) The three forms of the relation of (a) and (b), giving rise to the logic, ethics and esthetics of educational categories. Spring term.
4. *The Universal Law and Problem of Thinking.* Special movements of the mind in learning discriminated. (a) How to think objects into organic unity. (b) How to think objects into class unity. Fall term.
5. *The Logical and the Psychological Factors in Educational Method,* that is, the foregoing process modified by the psychological factor. (a) The sketching of the lessons in recognition of the two factors. (b) The course of study as determined by the two factors; the chronological and logical arrangement of studies. Winter term. [154]

In order to indicate more concretely the place of general theory courses in the evolving curriculum, the professional offerings of the University of Michigan are reported from the establishing of the department of education in 1879 to 1900. The first state university to organize a separate department of education, it tended more or less to set the pattern for other university departments of education that were being established during this period. [89:6, 98:114]

According to the founder, W. H. Payne, the department of education or "Science and Art of Teaching," as it was called, was organized to accomplish the following purposes (courses of a broadly theoretical nature are directly referred to in items 2 and 3):

1. To fit the university students for the higher positions in the public school service;
2. To promote a philosophic study of the educating art;
3. To teach the history of education and of educational systems and doctrines;
4. To secure to teaching the rights, prerogatives and advantages of a profession;
5. To give a more perfect unity to our State educational system by bringing the secondary schools into closer relations with the University. [155:44]

Two courses were offered this first year, one each semester. They are described as follows: "Practical; embracing school supervision, grading, courses of study, examinations, the art of instructing and governing, school architecture, school hygiene, school law, etc." "Historical, Philosophical and Critical; embracing history of education, the comparison and criticism of the systems in different countries, the outlines of educational science, the science of teaching, and a critical discussion of theories and methods." [155:45] In this offering of two courses, the one "practical" and the other "historical, philosophical and critical," it appears that the teaching of general educational theory occupied a relatively high place. The brief outline of the latter suggests a course intended to develop the broad outlook which is here held to be one of the chief functions of courses in general educational theory.

The second year the lecture plan of instruction was changed to the "study of a text, followed by lectures and recitations." Fitch's *Lectures on Teaching* was the text for the practical course; Bain's *Education as a Science* was the text for the theoretical course. [98:106 ff.]

The following year, two new courses were added, one on "School supervision," the other a seminary course for the study of educational classics. The books used in the latter course were Spencer's *Education*, Rousseau's *Emile*, and Laurie's *Life of Comenius*. The use of these texts would indicate a course which was definitely philosophical in nature.

By 1894-1895 the original set-up had been increased by the addition of such courses as history of education, now a course in its own right of two semesters, a course in comparative education, and a course called "The Great Exponents of Educational Thought and Practice."

By 1899-1900 the following courses were offered at Michigan. Course descriptions are included only with those courses that come closest to general educational theory.

First Semester

1. Practical Pedagogy.
3. History of Education, Ancient and Medieval. Recitation and lectures. Text-book: Compayré's History of Pedagogy. The subjects treated in the lectures are Oriental, Greek and Roman education, and the Rise and Early Development of Christian Schools. Three hours.
4. School Supervision.
9. Child Study.
10. Social Phases of Education. A consideration of the school as a social factor in its relation to the child, to the home, to the church and to the State; also a discussion of the relation of education to vocation and to crime. Lectures and recitations. Textbook: Dutton's Social Phases of Education. One hour.

Second Semester

2. Theoretical and Critical Pedagogy. The principles underlying the arts of teaching and governing. Lectures and readings. Hinsdale's Studies in Education. Four hours.

4. History of Modern Education. Recitations and lectures. Textbook: Compayré's History of Pedagogy. The topics to be dealt with in the lectures are the movements of modern educational thought and practice. Three hours.

6. The Comparative Study of Educational Systems, Domestic and Foreign. Lectures and reading. Two hours.

7. History of Education in the United States. The course deals with the salient features of the subject from the earliest time, but particular attention is paid to the state of education in the colonies, and to the common school revival in the first half of the present century. The recent university development is also described. Lectures and reading. Hinsdale's Horace Mann and the Common School Revival in the United States and Documents Illustrative of American Educational History, are subjects of examination. One hour.

8. History of Educational Thought. The course deals with Greek and Roman antiquity and the Middle Ages, and with the principle of the great movements of thought in modern times. Lectures and reading. Davidson's Aristotle and Ancient Educational Ideals, West's Alcuin and the Rise of Christian Schools, and Browning's Educational Theories, are principal books of reference. One hour.
[155:81-2]

Out of a total of ten courses given in 1899-1900 in this institution, seven seem to be sufficiently philosophical in nature to be counted as courses in general educational theory. The descriptions of the courses, and the texts mentioned point to the theoretical type of material which is the chief concern of this study.

Attention is called especially to course number 10, "Social Phases of Education." This course indicates the presence of a new emphasis in professional education. Previously, educational theory had been chiefly concerned with individual development. That this course was offered in 1899 shows that educational theorists were beginning to see the need for special study of education as related to society.

The first mention of such a course is to be found in the catalogue of New York University for 1889. Among the six courses offered in the education department was "Sociology, in so far as it has reference to education." [11:147] In 1893 W. T. Harris, one of the most influential educators of the day, urged such a course in a magazine article, "No philosophy of education is sound . . . unless based upon sociology." [132] Three years later he stated before the National Educational Association that "education was founded upon sociology." [97:1] The same year appeared "My Pedagogic Creed" by John Dewey, "The Demands of Sociology upon Pedagogy" by Albion W. Small, two articles printed together as one pamphlet. Both articles vigorously urged the social nature of education, and the necessity of preparing children for life in society. In 1897 appeared *Social Aspects of Moral Education* by Charles DeGarmo, and two years later two important works, *Social Phases of Education in School and Home* by S. T. Dutton (the text used at Michigan) and *School and Society* by John Dewey. By 1900 six universities offered courses in sociology which were designed for prospective teachers.

It is significant that these early efforts to relate sociology to education took place at universities. One reason may be that the universities, not concerned so much with methods of teaching as were the normal schools, tended to center more attention on the broader aspects of education. Also, their preoccupation with history of education and philosophy of education no doubt fostered interest in social problems. Another reason for offering sociology to teachers is likely to be found in the fact that sociology as a field of research had by this time made considerable progress, and was becoming an object for study in colleges and universities. As the study developed, the bearing of the school upon needed social reforms became more and more apparent. The actual presence of departments of education and sociology in the same institutions may have helped to bring the two together. This study of education in its broader social setting is one of the distinct contributions of the American university to teacher training.

A study made by Bolton [123] at the close of this period tends to corroborate all that has been reported as to the status of the more purely theoretical courses in the university departments of education. Bolton found from a questionnaire sent to all members of the newly organized National Society of College Teachers of Education that "the course most largely aimed at is history of education." Courses in philosophy and principles of education were the next most numerous class.

The situation in the normal schools at the close of this period is shown in the following table prepared by Ruediger after examining eighty normal-school catalogues. [146]

Subject	Number of Schools	Average Number of Weeks	Median Number of Weeks
Psychology	68	22.5	20.1
Pedagogics	54	16	12.5
History of education	65	15	12.7
School management	46	12	12
Methods and reviews	35	23.5	20.6

("Pedagogics" included principles of education and principles of teaching.)

It is seen that psychology was given in the greatest number of schools. That psychology, except for "methods and reviews," received the most time again gives evidence of the expansion of the more technical aspects of education which Luckey had found to be underway in the university departments of education by 1900. History of education next to psychology was found in the greatest number of schools, and pedagogics—a term used to include principles of education and principles of teaching—came next in order. The prevalence of history of education and the courses included under pedagogics shows that in the normal schools, as in the universities, the courses more definitely of a theoretical nature occupied an important place. As one might expect, however, there is less emphasis on the theoretical courses in the normal schools. Although principles of education included in the rubric pedagogics concerned itself to some extent with general educational theory, it stressed the practical or actual teaching procedures, and thus probably was not so highly theoretical as the courses listed by Luckey under such titles as philosophy of education, theory of education, or institutes of education.

During this period, 1880-1905, a large number of professional textbooks appeared, of which a few of the more widely used were examined for the purposes of this study. [95:151-59] These books reflect the varying educational philosophies of the time and are essentially of four types. The first type resembles the books of the previous period in that they follow somewhat the Pestalozzian—faculty psychology—object-teaching point of view. The second group, of which one text has been selected as typical, reflects the Hegelian philosophy. The third group is composed of books setting forth the Herbartian pedagogy, and the fourth group represents the pragmatic philosophy of education as developed by James and Dewey. All of these books, with the exception of the James-Dewey group, are of foreign origin or strongly influenced by foreign thought.

It is understood, of course, that the texts described in the previous section continued to be used to a greater or less degree in the early part of this period. To the extent that they were used, what was said of the teaching of general educational theory in Section II applies also here.

The books of the first type examined were: *Philosophy of Education or Principles and Practice of Teaching* by Thomas Tate (1884), *Lectures on the Science and Art of Education* by Joseph Payne (1884), *Education as a Science* by Alexander Bain (1879), *Lectures on Teaching* by J. G. Fitch (1885), *Lectures on Pedagogy: Theoretical and Practical* by Gabriel Compayré (1887), *Elements of Pedagogy* by E. E. White (1886).[23]

With the exception of White's *Elements of Pedagogy*, these were European books, four of them English and one French. Having been written some time before being introduced in America, several reflect an earlier point of view than was found in White's book. This book showed the weakening of the faculty psychology then in process. For example, the "soul" was said to be capable of three activities or "powers" instead of composed of a number of distinct faculties. [66:21] The discussion which followed was not essentially different from the texts based on faculty psychology.

These books, like those in Section II, contained considerable material not of a broadly theoretical nature, although the variety of topics treated was not so great. In common with the older books much space was given to such subjects as psychology, general methods and special methods of teaching the school subjects. Scant mention was made, however, of the "personal relationships of the teacher" or the principle of public support of education which by this time was generally established. School management was likewise omitted with one exception, this topic now being itself the subject of textbooks in education. The proportion of theoretical to non-theoretical material varied considerably. Payne's text, for example, was about 90 per cent philosophical, as we here use the term; Bain and Compayré approximately 40 per cent.

As has been stated before, the examination of books was undertaken with the belief that the nature and motives of general educational theory of the times would best be seen in the broader conception advanced through writing and teaching. They reveal at

---

[23] Date given is year of American edition. Tate was first published in 1854, Payne 1874, Bain 1879, Fitch 1881, Compayré 1885.

one and the same time the prevailing philosophy and the corresponding sense of the needs of the teacher.

The authors of this group of books thought educational theory important essentially for the same reasons as those discussed in Section II. Different emphases, however, were noted. The point at which these books differed most with the books of the preceding period was in the matter of religious and moral instruction. The religious atmosphere of the former books was gone.[24] The Deity was rarely mentioned and the theological conception of this life as a preparation for the life to come had been displaced by the idea that the practice of morality was justified by its effects on present life. W. H. Payne in his Preface to Compayré's *Lectures on Teaching*, which he translated, thus explained the latter's stand on the matter of religious education: "The public school is a civil institution, but on this account it is neither godless, unchristian, nor immoral. Between the church and the state there has come about a division of functions, and there is no good reason why they may not coöperate as honorable and helpful allies. This thought has never been more tersely and beautifully expressed than in these words by our author: 'We shall continue to build on our solid bases of justice, charity, and tolerance the human city, while leaving to the ministers of religion the task of building beside it what St. Augustine called the City of God.'" [18:iv]

According to these authors the teacher must understand that the school's part in building up morality was to be accomplished through the discipline of the school and through the force of his example rather than through religious instruction. Such a conception being at variance with what had formerly prevailed required in some measure a reconsideration of theories of morality and education. In a chapter on "Moral Education," Bain said, "The school master, in common with all persons exercising control for a particular purpose, is a moral teacher or disciplinarian; contributing his part to impress good and evil consequences in connection with conduct. . . . He enforces and cultivates obedience, punctuality, truthfulness, fair dealing, courteous and considerate behavior, and whatever else belongs to the working of the school." [5:401] He recommended that teachers show the evils of the various vices and the consequences of the virtues, the chief of which he described and classified. At the close of the chapter he made this statement: "We have viewed Morality hitherto without naming connection with Religion." He denied the

---
[24] The book by Tate written in 1854 was the one exception.

integral relationship of religion and morality and insisted the ends of each were "all the more effectively worked, when worked in separation." [5:421]

Fitch, at the end of his book, much after the manner of the other writers apologetically referred to his failure to mention the teaching of religion. "In all this, I have said nothing of religious and moral teaching. But this is not because I disregard it, but simply because it is impossible to coördinate it with any of the subjects of which we have spoken. To say, for example, that so many hours should be given to grammar, so many to science, and so many to Biblical or moral lessons, would be difficult, and would not, whatever the proportion of time assigned, rightly represent our estimate of the relative importance of this last element." Fitch also concluded that teaching religion was not necessarily essential to the development of moral character, but that the latter could be accomplished through "the moral lessons taught by the discipline of the school" and "the ethical teaching embodied in school lessons."[29:385-90]

Another point of difference between the books of this period and those of the previous period was the greater emphasis by the several writers on child activity. In advocating the use of objects in teaching the authors did not want the parroting of the teacher so characteristic of the formalized "object teaching." They insisted that the child must himself be active. [18:16-7] This concept must be due in some measure to the emphasis given child activity by the growing acceptance of Froebel's theories.

In describing the good teacher Payne said: "She makes her pupils learn to do by doing, to live by living. She gives him no grammar of seeing, hearing, etc.; she gives no compendiums of abstract principles. She would stop his progress at the very threshold, if she did. Action! action! is her maxim of training." [51:79]

Greater emphasis was given in these books to the conviction that the principles set forth constituted a science of education and that the teacher's first duty was to learn the principles of this science. Compayré said, "No one doubts today, the possibility of a science of education." [18:4] "My object," said Payne, "has been so forcibly to stamp upon their minds [teachers] a few great principles, so strongly to impress them with convictions of the truth of these principles, that it should be impossible, in the nature of things, for them to act in contradiction or violation of them." [51:34] Bain's book, bearing the significant title of *Education as a Science*, opened with the statement that "scientific treatment of any art consists partly in applying the principles furnished by the several sciences involved, as chemical laws to agriculture; and partly in enforcing, throughout the discussion, the utmost precision and rigour in the statement, deduction and proof of the various maxims or rules that make up the art." It may be said that the phrase "utmost precision and rigour of statement, deduction and proof of the various maxims" adequately characterizes Bain, Compayré, and White.

Also, these books differed from those previously discussed in their far greater emphasis on psychology as a need for teachers. They represented faculty psychology at its height. William H. Payne,[25] author of the Preface to the American edition of Compayré's book, said: "These lectures will commend themselves to that class of teachers, now rapidly growing in numbers, who are looking to psychology as the rational basis of their art. They will discover . . . that psychology is not an occult science, but that the main laws and essential facts of the individual can be expressed in intelligible terms." [18:iii] Bain and Compayré particularly exhausted the possibilities of the faculty psychology.

Likewise there was noted a difference in the way of presenting the aims of education. These authors seemed to feel that the teachers should know earlier aims of education and by noting their inadequacies develop a clear conception of what education should be. To this end considerable space was devoted to a criticism of various aims of other educational philosophers before arriving at a definition of their own. Compayré cited and criticized fifteen aims of education before phrasing a definition intended to escape the shortcomings of the other definitions. [18:9-13] Such an approach to the study of education must have had the effect of broadening, somewhat, the educational viewpoints of the students.

Attention is also called to an interesting feature of Payne's book—an effort to show the practicality of theory. "I am well aware that the mention of the words, 'Theory of Education,' and the assumption that the educator ought to be educated in it, is apt to excite some degree of opposition in the minds of those who claim especially the title of 'practical teachers,' and who therefore characterize this theory as 'a quackery.' . . . We agree with them as to the value, the indispensable value of the practical, but not as to the

---

[25] The first American instructor of education to enjoy the rank of professor, and founder of the department of education at the University of Michigan.

assumed antagonism between theory and practice. So far from being in any sense opposed, they are identical. Theory is the general, practice the particular expression of the same facts. . . . So, in Education, theory and practice go hand in hand; and the practical man who denounces theory is a theorist in fact." [51:44-5] Payne went on to argue that without theory, "without intellectual freedom," teachers were "slaves of routine," and were thus incapable of "emancipating their pupils." He concluded with the argument "that a man engaged in a profession, as distinguished from a mere handicraft, ought not only to know *what* he is doing, but *why*; the one constituting his practice, the other his theory. . . . Education can never take its proper rank among the learned professions . . . until teachers see that there are really principles of Education, and that it is their duty to study them." [51:45-50]

The philosophy of the Hegelians, reflected in the group of books representing the second type of general educational theory, can be understood more clearly by noting briefly certain aspects of the movement. The Hegelian movement first made itself felt in America through the work of William T. Harris, superintendent of the St. Louis city schools and for sixteen years United States Commissioner of Education. A man of versatile interests and of profound thought, he is considered by some to be one of the greatest scholars America has ever produced.[26] More than any other person up to that time, he generated interest in general and educational philosophy. Under his hand the "St. Louis school" in philosophy became a power in American thought[27] and the first metaphysical journal in the country, the *Journal of Speculative Philosophy*, which he edited from 1867 to 1893, was brought into being. [105:240] Unfortunately, Harris never prepared a complete statement of his philosophy; it is found only in isolated reports, magazine articles, and introductions to books written by others.

As editor of the International Education Series, he arranged the translation of Rosenkranz' highly metaphysical *Philosophy of Edu-*

[26] "I measure my words when I say that in my judgment, Dr. Harris had the one truly great philosophical mind that has yet appeared on the western continent." "Changes of a Quarter Century." [126]

As superintendent of schools, Harris was the first to incorporate in his system a public kindergarten and also the first to attempt to provide for individual differences by making the grading system more flexible. (By interview with Professor Bagley.)

[27] In 1889 Boone wrote that "the most complete and systematic presentation of educational philosophy" could be found in the annual reports of the St. Louis schools from 1867 to 1879. [11:155]

cation [55], from the German. More than any other book, it introduced into American education the concepts of Hegelian idealism, and as has been mentioned before, gave vogue to the term "philosophy of education" in American teacher-training institutions. Harris' own thought is closely identified with it for on nearly every page are his running comments on the text.

The need of a theoretical book for teachers, which this text was intended to fill, is set forth by Harris in the Editor's Preface as follows:

It is believed that the book as it now appears will meet a want that is widely felt for a thoroughgoing Philosophy of Education. There are many useful and valuable works on "The Theory and Practice of Teaching," but no work that entirely satisfies the description of a genuine Philosophy of Education. To earn this title, such a work must not only be systematic, but it must bring all its details to the test of the highest principles of philosophy. This principle is the acknowledged principle of Christian civilization, and as such, Rosenkranz makes it the very foundation of his theory of education, and demonstrates its very validity by an appeal to psychology on the one hand and to history of civilization on the other." [55: vi]

At the heart of this philosophy, which was based on the "acknowledged principle of Christian civilization," was the concept of dualism. This dualism or theory of "opposites" is revealed in the following: "Education comprehends, therefore, the reciprocal action of the opposites; authority and obedience; rationality and individuality; work and play; habit and spontaneity." [55:35]

Of first importance in this philosophy and an important reason for teaching general theory to prospective teachers was the matter of moral and religious education. Teachers should realize that religion is innate in human nature and comes from the Absolute. "The educator must not allow himself to suppose that he is able to make a religion. Religion dwells originally in every individual soul, for every one is born of God. Education can only aid the development of the religious feeling." [55:161] "Education must, therefore, first accustom the youth to the idea, that in doing good, he unites himself with God as with the absolute Person, but that in doing evil he separates himself from him." [55:169]

The proper moral habits were brought about by an "education of the will." "But in a narrower sense we mean by practical education, the methodical development of the will. . . . The will is already the subject of a science of its own, i.e., of ethics; . . ." [55:

141] This "education of the will" is to follow three lines of virtue: "(a) Social culture, or obedience to established customs; (b) Moral culture, or obedience to recognized good; (c) Religious culture, or obedience to spiritual laws." [55:289]

This insistence on "training the will" required a strong program of discipline. Successful teaching meant subduing the animal nature so that the "ideal" nature could be achieved. This was a theory of life which the teacher must comprehend. It was this principle that most aroused the opposition of the Herbartians. Rosenkranz called it the principle of "self-estrangement" (*Selbst-Entfremdung*) and Harris thus described it: "Since man's true nature is not found in him already realized at birth, but has to be developed by his activity, his true nature is his ideal, which he may actualize by education. . . . Man must estrange himself from his first or animal nature, and assimilate himself to his second or ideal nature, by habit. . . . Education begins when he puts aside what is familiar and customary with him, and puts on the new and strange—that is to say, begins his 'self-estrangement!'" [55:vii]

This self-estrangement meant that effort must be applied and that the individual's "own personal inclinations must be entirely subordinated, and the business that he is at work upon must be carried forward in accordance with its own ends and aims, and without reference to his own feelings in the matter." [55:30] "We must discipline ourselves constantly to form and to break habits, as a means toward the ever-developing realization of the good in us." [55:34] "The careful, persistent, living activity of the pupil in these acts we call industry. Its negative opposite is laziness, which is deserving of punishment inasmuch as it proceeds from a want of self-determination. Man is by nature lazy." [55:114]

To form these proper habits "work and play must be sharply distinguished from each other by the teacher. If one does not insist on respect for work as an important and substantial activity, he not only spoils play for the pupil (for this loses all its attraction when deprived of the antithesis of an earnest, set task) but undermines the respect for real existence. . . . Work should never be treated as if it were play, nor play as if it were work." [55:29-30]

In this philosophy obedience to duty, one of the highest virtues, must be cultivated in the schoolroom. "Thence follows the maxim relating to the idea of duty, that we must accustom the pupil to unconditional obedience to it, so that he shall perform it for no other reason than that it is his duty. The performance of a duty may bring with it externally a result agreeable or disagreeable, useful or harmful; but the consideration of such consequences ought never to determine us." [55:150-51]

Such concepts as these along with an exposition of psychology and a short history of education, "based on the philosophy of history," comprised the book. This last was "rather an outline of the history of human culture than a special history of schools or of pedagogics." Its chief purpose, it seemed, was to present Christianity as the one true world religion by comparing it with other religions of the world.

The distinction of presenting a systematic statement of philosophy of education in contrast with the empirical and common-sense type of material that was usually found in earlier textbooks in education probably goes to the Hegelians. Other books following in the same tradition are *Philosophy of School Management* by Arnold Tompkins (1895), *Principles of Education* by Malcolm MacVicar (1892), *Psychologic Foundations of Education* by W. T. Harris (1898), and *College Course in the Principles of Education* by John Angus MacVannel (1906).

The leaders of the Herbartian movement, which swept American education during the 90's much as the Oswego movement did during the 60's and 70's, were Charles DeGarmo and Frank and Charles McMurry. Fresh from Germany where Professors Rein and Ziller had fired them with an almost apostolic zeal for the pedagogy of Herbart, they proclaimed the new psychology and the new methodology with a vigor that was not even excelled by Edward Sheldon in his enthusiasms for object-teaching. Organized at first as the Herbart Club (1892), and later as the National Herbart Society (first yearbook, 1895), they made their work so effective that the normal schools adopted the Herbartian methods almost unanimously. [90:60] Their emphasis on the rôle of the teacher in the educative process, their insistence that the teacher understand their more rational psychology and technique of teaching added more prestige to professional teacher education and tended everywhere to strengthen the position of the normal schools and departments of education at the universities. With a new conception of teaching, the older theories were challenged and educators were required to reconstruct their theoretical position. The Herbartian movement was thus one of the contributing factors toward stimulating the extensive interest in educational philosophy during this period.

The curricula of these institutions were also modified, the most significant change being the creation of a new course, "General Method." Sometimes the title "Herbartian Pedagogy" was used.[28] Besides aiming to acquaint the student with the theory of Herbartian pedagogy, these courses presented the methodology which was summarized in the formula of the five formal steps. These steps, much in the same manner as object-teaching three decades before, were hailed as the "magic key" to success in teaching; their mastery was as important for teachers as shorthand for stenographers. Normal school students were compelled to memorize these five steps as in a later day they were required to memorize Thorndike's laws of learning. The requirement that student lesson plans follow this organization was even more significant.

Most of the textbooks written by the Herbartians were intended for the course, General Method. A few representative ones were examined for the purpose of this study: *Essentials of Method* by Charles DeGarmo (1889), *Elements of Method Based on the Principles of Herbart* by Charles A. McMurry (1893), *Herbart and the Herbartians* by Charles DeGarmo (1895). Among other things these books revealed the belief that the teacher must understand the nature of the mind. The Herbartians held that the mind was built through experience. According to this theory, called the "architectural theory," the nature of experience depended upon the environment. If the educator was to function as such, it was imperative that he appreciate the importance of the environment, which, as it determined the nature of experience, determined also the nature of the mind, and thus the very character of the individual. This conception DeGarmo described as "that theory which regards the mind at any given stage of its development, as a product more *externally* than *internally* produced." "The mind," he said, "is produced by the educational architect," and the teacher is thus an "architect of the mind." [22:3]

In this process the teacher was to be guided by the supreme aim of building moral character, an object of first importance to the state. McMurry wrote, "This is exactly the point at which we wish to apply the lever and to lift into prominence the *moral character-building* aim as the central one in education. This aim should be like a lodestone, attracting and subordinating all other purposes to itself. It should dominate in the choice, arrangement, and method of studies. . . . Again the *state* is more concerned to see the growth

[28] Given at the University of North Carolina (1894-95), and at the University of Michigan during the 90's and early 1900's. [98:27]

of just and virtuous citizens than in seeing the prosperity of scholars, inventors, and merchants. . . . Our country may have vast resources and great opportunities, but everything in the end depends upon the *moral quality* of its men and women." [43:10]

Based on this conception of the nature of the individual were certain conceptions of the nature of learning which the teacher must know. Most important of these was the doctrine of interest. Genuine learning took place only when the child was interested in the new object and actually wanted to learn about it. "By interest we mean the natural attractiveness of the subject that draws and holds the attention. . . . Interest keeps the mind active and alert without undue excitement or partiality." [43:61]

"Interest is a very practical thing. It is that which gives force and momentum to ideas. It is not knowledge itself, but, like the invisible principles of life, it converts dead matter into living energy. In our schools thus far we have had too much faith in the mechanics of education. Too much virtue has been imputed to facts, to knowledge, to sharp tools. We have now to learn that *incentive* is a more important thing in education; that is, a direct, permanent, many sided interest." [43:85]

Whether or not a subject would be interesting depended very much upon the technique of the teacher. He must know how to present the material so as to attract the interest of the student. This meant building on the past experience of the child or the "apperceptive mass," as the Herbartians called it. "We have seen how apperception, or the subsumption of new subjects under the old predicates, is the condition of all *interest*, for the mind has no interest in that which it does not understand. . . . There are, therefore, two powerful incentives for the teacher to study the conditions of apperception,—the desire to have his pupils comprehend, and the desire to have them interested." [22:45]

Other educational theories which the teacher must understand, according to the Herbartians, were the culture epoch theory, the principle of correlation of subject matter, and the tenet of the peculiar value of the social studies in moral education. But it was their doctrine of interest which attracted most attention and which brought them into conflict with the Hegelians with their opposing theory of effort.

The struggle for supremacy between these two contrasting philosophies as to whether interest or effort should constitute the basis of the learning process made the 90's interesting in the field of educational discussion and controversy; and it was this situation that furnished an opportunity for Dewey's dramatic resolution of the conflict. In 1896 his *Interest in Relation to the Training of the Will*, later revised as *Interest and Effort in Education*, demonstrated that both sides were wrong in their common assumption of "externality" of the object to be learned. This work contributed toward the deflation of Herbartianism in the United States. Note the change of the National Herbart Society in 1902 to the National Society for the Scientific Study of Education. This may be due partially to Dewey's early influence.

The publishing of this book marked the advent of a new philosophy of education. This philosophy, which represents the fourth main stream of thought of the period and which, unlike the others, was largely indigenous [75:I] to America, is often called pragmatism.[29] It is the result of the combined contributions of Charles Sanders Peirce, William James, and John Dewey. [105:280]

As professor of philosophy and director of the school of education at the University of Chicago from 1896 to 1903, and as author of such significant works as *My Pedagogic Creed, Interest in Relation to the Training of the Will,* and *School and Society,* Dewey brought to the study of education a fresh viewpoint as to the relation of the individual and society in education. It is to Dewey that we owe the formulation of the educational implications of this philosophy. These early pronouncements pointed to the social nature of the educative process, and to the consequent necessity of breaking down the isolation of the school from society by providing in the school an environment for social experience, and on the other hand to the belief that the school should so develop the child that he "will have the full and ready use of all his capacities." [26:7] The teacher, he urged, must understand the importance of building in the children a flexible intelligence capable of meeting the needs of changing social conditions. This intelligence was best developed by allowing considerable freedom in the school, freedom to move about and freedom to exercise initiative. The teacher must realize that he was engaged, not only in the educating of individuals "but in the formation of the proper social life." [26:17] Education he held "is the fundamental method of social progress and reform." [26:15]

The social emphasis was especially clear in *My Pedagogic Creed* and *School and Society.* They mark the beginning of an emphasis

[29] Dewey himself does not often use the word pragmatism.

which later was to occupy a significant place in courses in educational theory and in education generally. Since this period marked only the beginning of Dewey's work as an educational theorist, the effect of his work on the teaching of general educational theory will be more completely seen in the next period.

The texts used for history of education in this period were far more philosophical than the texts of the previous period, although the book by Hailman did anticipate this philosophical interest. His book especially maintained its popularity for a long time; a new edition appeared in 1894 under the title *History of Education*. Among the most widely used texts in history of education written during this period are: *Essays of Educational Reformers* by R. H. Quick (1885), *History of Pedagogy* by Gabriel Compayré (1885), *History of Education* by F. V. N. Painter (1886), *Education in the United States, Its History from the Earliest Settlements* by R. G. Boone (1889), *History of Modern Education* by S. G. Williams (1892), *A History of Education* by Thomas Davidson (1900).

The books examined for this study were those of Quick, Compayré, Williams, Davidson, and Boone. Except for the last one mentioned, these books were chiefly concerned with the various historic philosophies as they affected education. In the minds of these writers success in teaching depended to a large extent upon a thorough understanding of the different educational philosophies, their advantages and disadvantages. Boone's book, on the other hand, was chiefly a record of the development of the American public school system. It is filled with details showing how public education got started in the colonies, how the colleges were established, how laws were passed in the various states for the support of elementary and secondary schools and for compulsory attendance, and other matters of like nature. Its purpose was clearly to present facts about education rather than to trace the development of educational theory.

While Quick's *Educational Reformers* gave many details of the lives of educational philosophers, it laid chief emphasis on their educational theories. It was written out of a belief that the best way to prepare teachers was to help them develop a philosophy of education by studying the "chief authorities" in education. "I venture to think, therefore, that practical men in education, as in most other things, may derive benefit from the knowledge of what has already been said and done by the leading men engaged in it, both past and present." [53:iv]

Compayré's *History of Pedagogy* was much more complete in scope and intensive in treatment, written to be studied "not for the purposes of erudition or for mere curiosity, but with a practical purpose for the sake of finding in it the permanent truths which are the essentials of a definite theory of education." In his introduction Compayré said, ". . . history of pedagogy . . . is closely connected with the general history of thought and also with the philosophic explication of human actions. . . . On the one hand they [pedagogical doctrines] have their causes and their principles in moral, religious, and political beliefs, of which they are the faithful image; on the other, they are instrumental in the training of the mind and in the formation of manners. Back of the *Ratio Studiorum* of the Jesuits, back of the *Émile* of Rousseau, there distinctly appears a complete religion, a complete philosophy." [17:xvii]

Equally philosophical, though more readable, are the books by Williams and Davidson. Like Quick and Compayré, most emphasis is devoted to the educational theories of the leading reformers. Luckey, writing in 1903, characterized Davidson's book as " 'A History of Education,' which might have been designated more appropriately, a history of the philosophy of education." [98:155]

Davidson, following Spencer's famous definition of evolution, thus defined his conception of history of education: "Education is conscious or voluntary evolution. Hence, history of education is a record of such evolution, and begins at the point where man takes himself into his own hand, so to speak, and seeks to guide his life toward an ever more definite, coherent heterogeneity, which is what we mean by his ideal end." [21:1-2]

Because, then, of the philosophical content of the most widely used texts of the period, it would seem that as a course history of education was intended to liberalize and broaden points of view by presenting varying and conflicting theories of education, by tracing the development of educational theories, and by introducing to the student the ideas of the best thinkers, past and present. In so far as this is sought, rather than the mere memorization of the facts of educational history, the course becomes in fact a course in general educational theory.

SECTION IV

THE TEACHING OF GENERAL EDUCATIONAL THEORY

FROM 1905 TO 1930

During no period was there such intimate interplay between our national experience and our educational theory as during the two and a half decades under treatment in the present section. In the period intervening between the rise of America to nationhood and the Civil War, a period during which public education succeeded in finding roots in the soil of American life, very little attention was given to general theory in professional courses for teachers. Of course, educational practice was based on certain notions of the good life, and on conceptions of human nature, society, and the universe. However, so uncritically were these notions and conceptions held that educators were hardly conscious of them as theories. The other two periods, that between the Civil War and 1880 and the one between 1880 and 1905, mark an ever-increasing growth in importance of the rôle of educational theory in teacher-training. The particular theories underlying the practice of education during these periods and constituting the substance of theory teaching in training institutions for teachers do not to a very important extent reflect the subject matter of American experience. They were basically foreign importations.

During the first of these periods a vague notion of "science," nature, psychology, in combination with a few principles of method supposed to be rooted in Pestalozzian pedagogy constituted the core of educational theory. While the period between 1880 and 1905 was characterized by an interest in theory in proportion to other phases of education, hitherto unequaled and since then unsurpassed in the history of American education, educational thought had in the main made no advance toward an organic relationship with the pattern of American life. The transcendentalism of Rosenkranz, the mysticism of Froebel, and the metaphysical character of Herbart's psychology did not reflect the experience of a people who were busily engaged in pushing back the frontier, building railroads, establishing industrial plants, and boasting of their practicality. It was only toward the end of this period that an indigenous philosophy of education began to emerge—the philosophy of John Dewey. The recognition of education as a "fundamental method of social progress and reform," and the insistence that significant education was a process of social experiencing and experimenting reflected the ideals of democracy, and the characteristics of American pioneering experience.

By 1905 the supremacy of the theories of education derived from the metaphysical conceptions of Froebel, Herbart, and the Hegelians was definitely challenged. The main contestant was the aims, values, and procedures derived from science and industry. The impact of science and industry on education will constitute the theme of the present section. For the present it should be noted that the influence of Dewey, too, contributed considerably to the undermining of the metaphysical foundations of education, although it was possibly not so effective as the scientific-industrial outlook in transforming the texture of educational practice.

In the course of the period considered in the present section Dewey's thinking developed in directions of greater clarity and pertinence to the problems in American life and education and brought about many changes especially toward the end of the period in educational theory and practice. None the less it fell short of effecting a basic transformation in American education. It gave impulse to significant but isolated educational experiments. It constituted the basic philosophical creed taught in a number of prominent universities. It was a continuous stimulus in the quest for an education that could significantly contribute to the good life in its individual and social aspects. But it did not materially modify teacher-training curricula.

That the Dewey influence had not made itself felt to a greater extent was due to the force of events unfolding themselves during this period. The movement of American history during the period under consideration had resulted in the emergence of values, attitudes, ideas, ways of doing things, which in their totality were far more effective in shaping active educational theory—the theory actually underlying the educational practice—than the philosophy of Dewey. One aspect of the American experience—industrialism and its correlate science—because of its remarkable strides of progress had pushed everything else into the background. That industrialism could have established an almost complete hegemony over education was due also to the fact that no American culture was as yet established to take the place of the European culture with which our people in settling the new continent had broken.

The outstanding fact of the period is the acceleration in the material growth of the country. Rapid as urbanization and industrialization were in the period between 1880 and 1905, they were slight as compared to the advance made during the decades of the twentieth century. This advance was made possible by the scientific achievements already available and by the steady pushing forward of the scientific horizon. Science and industry came to be more and more organically related. Each stimulated the other. Each facilitated the other's progress. Size, bigness, speed, volume, practical usefulness were the basic ideals of the people. The "bigger and better idea" was expressed in the development of vast industries, in the digging of the Panama Canal, in huge financial enterprises in Latin America and in the Orient, in the enormous undertakings occasioned by the World War, in the unprecedented production of goods of the 20's, in the erection of gigantic skyscrapers, in the speeding up of transportation, and in the great corporations that in time came to control the economic life of the nation. Methods of observation and experimentation became more refined; instruments of measurement more precise. The areas of control over natural forces greatly expanded. The American people were convinced that they were advancing rapidly toward the kingdom of a material heaven. From this conviction there grew a new religion—the worship of science and industry. The methods and goals of these two forces served as the matrix for all human values and as models for conducting affairs in all areas of human life.

Naturally educational theory, too, reflected our industry and science. It is only in terms of scientific techniques and scientific method that the tendencies in educational theory and practice in this period are fully intelligible. Hitherto educational theory had been grounded in academic philosophy. Among the considerations taken into account by the educator were the nature of the universe and the destiny of man. In the universities education had been under the tutelage of philosophy departments. But as the period advanced the break between education and philosophy became more pronounced. Instead a close alliance was established with psychology which by this time had become transformed and itself was under the sway of the physical sciences. No longer was the psychologist concerned with the soul or consciousness. The new subject matter of psychology was "behavior," "S—R bonds," "response mechanisms," "behavior patterns," etc. Increasingly precise measurement and controlled experimentation came to take the place of introspection and qualitative studies. It was this reconstructed psychology that came to be the basis of education.

Significant of the new alignment of educational thought are the observations of Judd made when he became head of the Department of Education at the University of Chicago. Up to this time the Departments of Philosophy and Education had been combined under one head, but when Judd assumed office the Department of Education became an independent department. "The history of the relation between philosophy and education in this institution is the same as it has been in general. The first efforts to stimulate educational ideals were made by the students of systematic philosophy. . . . Psychology had in the interval grown into a distinct department and had contributed much in courses and general support to the training of teachers and supervisors. The establishment of a Department of Education does not mark a breach in earlier intimate relations; . . . [it] marks the recognition of the necessity of specialized scientific study of educational problems." [134]

A pioneer of the new psychology in America was William James. His *Principles of Psychology*, which appeared in 1890, marks a clear break with *a priori* psychology. In this work "faculties" are thrown overboard, "instinct" makes way for specific instincts, a greater emphasis on physiology is noticeable, and habit formation comes in for considerable attention. It emphasized more precise observation and scientifically controlled experimentation. The influence of James coupled with that of several Americans who had studied psychology in German universities, especially under Wundt, was mostly responsible for the "scientific" nature of contemporary psychology. Among the students of Wundt was G. Stanley Hall, who at the beginning of the period under consideration was engaged in writing his *Adolescence*. Another student of Wundt was James McKeen Cattell. It was during his German student days that Cattell began experimenting in the hitherto unknown field of intelligence testing. It is related that when Wundt was informed of this project he commented, "Das ist ganzlich Amerikanisch" (This is completely American), referring to the practical inspiration underlying intelligence testing. Thorndike and Cattell established psychological laboratories and with Goddard, Terman, and Childs developed the technique of intelligence testing which in time came to be an important element in teacher-training programs. [73:494-522]

Bringing psychology more directly to education, Thorndike established the course, "Educational Psychology." The final formulation of this course in the three-volume *Educational Psychology* is one of the most important events in the educational history of this period. The course and the books based on it signify more than anything else the character education assumed. Hitherto psychology was applied more or less externally to education. In Thorndike's conception psychology is at the root of educational practice. Just as dynamics and statics constitute the theory of engineering, so does psychology constitute the theory of education. The scope of educational psychology embraces the facts of the material upon which education works: "original nature," the mechanics of its transformation—the laws of learning, and the measurement of the material subject to education and the changes effected therein by education—"individual differences." [111] The assumptions of the physical sciences are in clear evidence throughout the book—that quality is reducible to quantity, that the material of education is reducible to units, S—R bonds, and that changes effected by education can be measured—are central in Thorndike's teaching. Under the influence of Thorndike and others the testing movement reached a position of importance which tended far to overshadow other branches of activity in the professional field.

In this manner in the early part of the century psychology was being reduced to what purported to be an exact science in the minds of the researchers, and education to an applied science. The remarkable faith in the predictions which educators felt could be made as the result of future investigation into the field of psychology is illustrated in the following statement made by Thorndike in 1910:

"A complete science of psychology would tell us every fact about everyone's intellect and character and behavior, would tell us the cause of every change in human nature, would tell the result which every educational force—every act of every person that changed any other or the agent himself—would have. It would aid us to use human beings for the world's welfare with the same surety of the result that we now have when we use falling bodies or chemical elements. In proportion as we get to such a science we shall become masters of our own souls as we now are masters of heat and light. Progress toward such a science is being made." [153]

Like medicine, education was thought to require only mastery of its scientific techniques. "The science of education," George D. Strayer said in 1911, "will in its development occupy relatively the same position with reference to the art of teaching that the science of medicine occupies with respect to the art of healing." [109:247]

Twenty years later we still find this conviction that scientific subject matter and scientific procedures constitute the chief basis for the practice of education. In 1931 David Snedden writes:

"What American educators now greatly desire is that in their fields of work they can begin to apply the findings of the sciences, from any and all sources, and to develop scientific procedures of their own whereby, as in the other great fields of enterprise named, they can rise to planes of efficiency impossible of realization so long as progress takes place on 'art levels' through 'Trial and error' methods only. . . . Many of us believe that even at the end of the first quarter of the twentieth century we educators stand at the threshold of quantitative achievements in education such as could hardly have been imagined at the opening of the century." [108: 1-2]

Not only did the new science of education claim to show the teacher *how* to teach, and how to *measure* what he taught, but it also claimed the power to decide *what* to teach. Not only the means but the ends of education were to be arrived at scientifically. Through the scientific techniques of "job analysis" and "activity analysis," Charters and Bobbitt believed the purposes of education and the content of the curriculum could be determined, and made practical.

Besides adopting the ideals of exact science, education again reflected the spirit of the times by adopting the ideals of big business. The passion for size, growth, business efficiency was expressed in the consolidation of school districts, in the erection of huge school buildings, which significantly were called "plants," in the development of elaborate systems of business and pupil accounting. The school, like the factory, was to be run on "business principles." Education was "practical" in a very narrow sense, thus reflecting a "practical" American civilization. The desire for "quick returns" predominated in education as well as in business. As Münsterberg pointed out, educators were concerned with means, "immediate objectives, rather than with the ends of education." The effort to fit the school into the business world is reflected in the rise and spread of the vocational guidance and training movement and in the rapid multiplication of specialized courses in the curriculum. As the period advanced, education was more and more dominated by the spirit of industry and business. "Efficiency" in the sense of mechanical adjustment to shop, office, and sales gang became a dominant educational ideal.

Teacher-training institutions reacted to these forces mentioned above. A theory of teacher training emerged which corresponded to the notion that it is the chief task of education to "fix" the traits and knowledges necessary to the "efficient" conduct of *status quo* industrial civilization. A statistical analysis of the atomic factors that enter into the teacher's job was thought quite sufficient for the purpose of formulating the ends and means, the curriculum, and method of a teacher-training program. Illustrative of this conviction are the following excerpts:

Until every program of curriculum for the training of teachers (of whatever species) is based upon clearly defined, factored, and evaluated job analyses of the specific responsibilities likely or desirably to be met, such curriculums will be excessively aspirational, general, bewildering to candidates, and relatively unfruitful of good to American education. [149]

To summarize: Curriculum building is like bridge building. Specify what the products of the curriculum must be. Then analyze these specifications of results to be achieved, and determine for each particular object and each particular type of teacher, what must be done in order that specifications may be fulfilled. This process will yield a curriculum that can be justified. Through it will run a unity derived not from a classification by subjects or departments, but from the inherent unity of the job itself. [138]

The crowning achievement of this trend of thought was the *Commonwealth Study of Teacher Training* by Charters and Waples, in which 1,001 specific teacher activities are offered as a basis for teacher-training programs.

Under the impact of this "scientific" spirit in teacher training, courses that had for their purpose the opening up of broader problems of education gradually lost ground. In the degree that education became scientific, teacher-training institutions tended to stress the "scientific" type of course at the expense of the philosophical. "With the behavioristic point of view now becoming dominant," John B. Watson wrote, "it is hard to find a place for what has been called philosophy. Philosophy is passing—has already all but passed." [158] In a similar vein wrote T. L. Kelley. ". . . there is but one method tending to establish truth in the world of phenomena. The more completely the philosopher parallels in his thinking the analysis and synthesis which the experimental treatment would yield the better is his philosophic solution. The great endeavor of the philosopher here should be to ape mentally the steps of science." [136]

As theoretical courses gradually lost ground in the teacher-training curriculum, courses in psychology, educational measurements, intelligence testing, educational statistics, curriculum building, and in the various branches of administration—school finance, budgetary procedures, taxation, etc.—increasingly grew in importance. After a comparison of the data obtained in his two studies made respectively in 1906 and 1914 of the curricula in university departments of education, Bolton concludes:

"There is a very definite tendency toward making all of the work in education more concrete and scientific and less abstractly theoretical. . . . In most of the universities experimental work and statistical methods are given a place. Not only are these considered in special courses, but the applications are finding their way into many of the theoretical courses." [121]

In the previous section, the curricular offerings of the department of education at the University of Michigan were discussed. The attention given to theory courses was noted. The 1922-1923 announcement indicates that since 1900 the relative importance of educational theory had considerably declined.

I. *History and Principles of Education*

101. The History of Ancient and Medieval Education.
102. The History of Education in the United States.
103. The History of Modern Education.
106. Principles of Education.
114. Social Education (omitted in 1922-1923).
201. Seminary in History of Education.

II. *Educational Administration and Supervision*

101. School Administration and Supervision.
201. Seminary in Administration.

III. *Secondary Education*

  1. Introduction to Secondary School Problems.
  4. Observation and Special Methods.
       (Choice of ten secondary school subjects)
101. Principles of Teaching in Secondary Schools.
102. The High School Curriculum.
103. The Junior High School.
104. Administration of Secondary Schools.
105. School Systems of Other Lands.
106. Administrative Problems of the Large High School.
210. Seminary in Secondary Problems.

IV. *Elementary Education*

 10. Educational Measurements in Elementary Education.
101. Psychology of Common School Branches.

103. Administration and Use of Tests in Elementary Education.
105. Principles Involved in the Project Method.
120. Methods of Instruction.
125. Seminary in Elementary Education.

V. Educational Psychology

1. Psychology of Education.
101. Psychology and Education of Exceptional Children.
102. Seminary in Educational Psychology (omitted in 1922-1923).
103. Problems in Educational Psychology.

VI. Educational and Mental Measurements

1. Introduction to Mental Testing.
101. Intelligence Testing.
102. Educational Statistics (omitted in 1922-1923).
110. Advanced Educational Measurements (omitted in 1922-1923).
210. Problems in Experimental Education.

VII. Industrial Education

1. Introduction to Vocational Education.
101. Vocational Guidance and Placement.
102. Social and Economic Background of Vocational Education
103. Methods of Teaching Industrial Subjects.
104. Compulsory Part-Time Schools.
105. Problems in Vocational Education.
106. Problems in Vocational Guidance.

VIII. Physical Education, Hygiene and Athletics [155: 585-603]

The six courses found in Group I represent the more or less theoretical courses. As against this group there are seven other groups of specialized and technical courses with a total of thirty-three courses.[30] The trend away from general theory may not be so pronounced as this comparison may suggest, however, for the following specialized courses may have included material of a broadly theoretical nature: Introduction to Secondary School Problems, Principles of Teaching in Secondary Schools, The High School Curriculum, School Systems in Other Lands, Principles Involved in the Project Method, and Social and Economic Background of Vocational Education. Even after these allowances have been made, the greater emphasis upon technical and specialized courses is clear.

The tendency for technical and specialized courses to displace the theoretical courses is shown by an examination of trends in teacher-

[30] The courses in Group VIII in Physical Education were not listed.

training curricula during 1902-1922 in both the two-year and the four-year institutions, as shown by Deyoe. [82:75] In the part of Deyoe's study devoted to prescribed courses in two-year curricula, the following trends in the general theory courses were noted. The prescription of general methods and principles of teaching dropped from 82 per cent to 54 per cent, history of education from 89 per cent to 29 per cent, philosophy and/or principles of education from 27 per cent to 20 per cent, professional ethics from 14 per cent to 7 per cent. Theory and art of teaching required in 18 per cent of the schools in 1902 was no longer required by 1922. Against this decline of general courses the increase of the technical, practical, and specialized courses was noted as follows: the requirement of observation and practice teaching increased in 1912 from 91 per cent to 100 per cent of the institutions examined; general and educational psychology increased from 95 per cent to 100 per cent; the percentage of institutions requiring such courses as child, adolescent, and genetic psychology increased from 14 to 20. By 1922 another type of psychology course had appeared among the required subjects—psychology of elementary subjects. Five per cent of the institutions studied included it in the required list. Tests and measurements rose suddenly in importance, being required in 22 per cent of the schools examined. Thus we note a decline in the relative place given to the theoretical subjects and an increase in the rôle of scientific and technical courses.

Similar trends were noted in prescribed courses for the four-year teachers colleges. [82:76] General methods and principles of teaching dropped in the twenty-year period from 71 per cent to 61 per cent; history of education from 86 per cent to 52 per cent; philosophy and/or principles of education from 43 per cent to 30 per cent; theory and art of teaching was no longer required in any of the institutions examined. On the other hand, scientific and technical subjects either maintained or improved their position. Educational psychology continued to be required in 100 per cent of the schools. The technical courses increased as follows: administration and supervision from 14 per cent to 17 per cent; observation and practice teaching from 86 per cent to 100 per cent. Child, adolescent, and genetic psychology and psychology of high school subjects made their appearance as required subjects for the first time in 1922 and were required in 13 per cent and 22 per cent of the schools respectively. Similarly, tests and measurements not before required were now prescribed in 26 per cent of the schools. Reflecting still further the increasing emphasis on the technical courses is the emergence of the course on "curriculum" required in 1922 in 4 per cent of the teachers colleges. The increase of specialization is noted in the rise of the new course, "principles of secondary education," required in 3 per cent of the colleges in 1922.

Educational sociology as such is not listed in Deyoe's tables, but attention is called in the text to the increasing requirement of sociology with "educational adaptations." A survey of teacher-training institutions by Keith [135] shows that as early as 1914 educational sociology had emerged from the field of general sociology. At this time ten universities required educational sociology of all students of education. In 1926 Lee [97:7] discovered that 48 normal schools, 13 teachers colleges, and 141 colleges and universities offered educational sociology. Begun just before the World War, the course speedily advanced. The growing complexity of society brought the realization on the one hand that the school was taking over the functions that previously belonged to other institutions and on the other hand that the school is only one among other educative institutions.

It is difficult to characterize the course in educational sociology. Clow [127] found four chief approaches to the course : (1) description and analysis of social phases of education; (2) education as a form of social activity; (3) principles of sociology with educational corollaries; (4) educational sociology as a distinct science. He further mentions that if the future "depended on the urgency with which these plans are advocated" the teaching of sociology as a distinct science would lead all the others. It would not be far from right to say, then, that a large number of courses were not concerned with examining the basic patterns of American life and the assumptions on which it was based; rather it was the aim to adjust education to existing social conditions. The school was conceived as a "coordinating" educative agency not the reconstructive educating agency. The common opinion of the times that statistical analysis of the *status quo* was adequate for the purpose is expressed in some of the educational sociology books published during this period. We find educational sociology books like Peters' [52] drawing heavily upon the job analysis of Charters and Bobbitt. A text enjoying much popularity was Snedden's *Educational Sociology* (1922). Accepting the *status quo*, he conceived the problem to be: What educational program is desirable for a certain individual or group? The solution to the problem was to be found by investigating the social situation in which the individual finds himself and by determining what demands that situation would make upon him.

It has been shown that history of education up to the turn of the century was chiefly concerned with the history of the philosophy of education and as such was a course in the general theory of education. However, as a factor in the development of broad general theories of education in professional curricula, this course for two reasons has played a diminishing rôle: (1) the decline of the importance of the course in professional curricula as shown by Deyoe's study;[31] (2) the change of emphasis in textbooks in the history of education from evolution of general educational theory to such aspects as the development of tax-supported schools, the machinery of public school control, the development of such specialized phases of education as vocational education, secondary education, higher education. [20] However, the course as now taught does include the development and introduction of the educational philosophies of such educational pioneers as Comenius, Locke, Rousseau, Pestalozzi, Herbart, Froebel, Harris, Parker, and Dewey. To the extent this course aims consciously to develop in the minds of the students conceptions of the meaning of education by the study of the' educational philosophies represented by the above names, it is a broadly theoretical course.

Again it was necessary, in order to gain a better understanding of the status of the teaching of general educational theory, to examine some of the textbooks that were in use during this period. While books of the type described in Section III continued to be used for some time, a great number of new books appeared of which a few were selected for examination. Some of these new books were examined, not for the purpose of reporting the prevailing educational philosophies of the period but rather to discover what factors within them most directly throw light on the teaching of educational theory. As brought out before, the textbooks reveal at the same time the prevailing philosophies and the corresponding sense of the needs of the teacher to develop his own philosophical outlook.

The books of this period may be roughly grouped in three classes: (1) books continuing the Hegelian tradition, of which H. H. Horne was the chief spokesman; (2) books reflecting the new scientific-biological-psychological emphasis, and (3) books reflecting the Dewey outlook and the books contributed by Dewey himself.

[31] In two-year curricula history of education dropped from 89 per cent in 1902 to 29 per cent in 1922; in four-year curricula from 86 per cent in 1902 to 52 per cent in 1922.

Of the first type, *Philosophy of Education* by H. H. Horne in its 1905 and 1927 editions was selected. Horne fell heir to the task of continuing the Hegelian idealism of W. T. Harris, and examination of his books shows that his general educational theory is based on philosophic views essentially similar to those of Rosenkranz. Because of their basically similar outlooks on life, their conceptions of the needs of the teacher were in essential agreement. In the first edition of Horne's book are found the same dualistic opposites of body and mind, culture and vocation, work and play, teacher and pupil we have noted in Rosenkranz. Also, the same religious emphasis based on what Horne called "idealistic theism" is central in thought. According to this view, "God is the self-conscious unity of all reality. Within His life falls the life of Nature and of man. We are the content of His consciousness." [37:269] By this time books of the Hegelian tradition were by far the most active in urging religious loyalties which were so prominent in education textbooks before 1880.

The conviction that the teacher must comprehend the philosophy of theistic idealism is clear. The teacher should realize that "without the assumption of an immanent Mind, all things—Nature, man, and his history—are meaningless. With this assumption, all things are shot through with infinite meaning, and life is the process of its interpretation. The race is working out its salvation with fear and trembling. For it is God that worketh in it both to will and to do His good pleasure." [37:134]

The need for a consideration of general educational theory is most deeply felt by those who hold positions significantly different from other prevailing positions. A conflict of views is the reason for concern with theories. One problem on which there was conflict at the time under consideration was the relation of interest and effort in education. We find in Horne's book a partial acceptance of the doctrine of interest, but true to his Hegelian tradition, the doctrine of "self-estrangement" is the core of his philosophy. That he gave a larger place to the discussion of interest than did Rosenkranz is due in large part to the challenges presented by the Herbartians and John Dewey. Horne said: "Interest is one of the great words in education, because it removes drudgery from the school, puts the motive power of the feelings at the disposition of the teacher, and is the immediate aim of all instruction." [37:191] But in common with Rosenkranz, he conceived the inculcation of the doctrine of self-estrangement as the primary purpose of philosophy of education. He does not, however, use the term "self-estrangement." Rather, he speaks of "self-realization." "Through the energy of effortful attention man becomes in his education what he is intended to be; he realizes his nature; develops his natural potentialities; attains his mental majority; declares his intellectual independence; . . . becomes a free being." [37:276]

Horne thus with Rosenkranz and Harris believed in the need for large stress on effort in education. "Education is the product of the mind's effort." [37:273] He defined effort as the "strain consciousness puts upon itself in performing unattractive work. It is voluntary attention to the uninteresting. It is the will to do one's duty when one doesn't want to." [37:199] Teachers must realize that "pupils should be taught that the struggle of strength is developed by doing what they do not like to do. In fact, not to want to do a given thing, not in itself bad, is itself a good reason for sometimes doing it. . . . Teachers and pupils must understand the nature of concentrated attention through effort." [37:202-03]

In typical Hegelian fashion, Horne made the following synthesis of the two rival positions of interest versus effort: "And our last word about effort and interest shall be this; it is only when they help each other that our work approaches perfection. To be interested without effort is to be entertained, to float with the current; to exert effort without interest is to be wearied, to row against the current; but to be interested with effort is to enjoy what is being accomplished, is to be steering for my destination while the current favors my progress." [37:206]

The 1927 revision of Horne's book is practically identical with the first book except for an additional chapter on "Pragmatism vs. Idealism." The inclusion of this chapter is suggestive of the growing importance of the pragmatic school of philosophy. Evidently the strength of the pragmatic naturalistic school of thought in education has stimulated much of Horne's interest in educational philosophy.

As illustrative of the second type, two books, *Principles of Education* by Frederick E. Bolton (1910) and *Educational Values* by William C. Bagley (1911), were examined. The former emphasized the conviction that teachers must understand scientific psychology and its biological basis and the latter the adjustment of the individual to society. By a use of books of this type, especially the former, in principles or philosophy of education these courses show a pronounced trend from an earlier connection with academic philosophy to a scientific-biological basis. Some of the chapters in Bolton's book read as if taken from texts in general or educational psychology.[32] The scientific emphasis is thus announced in the Preface: "The chief claim made for this book is that it assembles the main, well-tested results of the scientific study of education from the psychological and biological viewpoints and presents them in a way which secures continuity, correlation, and a unified interpretation of them." [10:viii]

Early in his book Bolton urged that the teacher should study the child. To him studying education without considering the child was like studying *"Hamlet* with Hamlet left out." "The latter part of the nineteenth century deserves lasting credit for centering the attention of educators upon the child instead of the curricula." [10:8]

Both writers felt the teacher should recognize education as a process of adjustment. From a biological point of view they perceived all living organisms in process of adjustment or adaptation to their environment. The human organism, likewise, has adjustments to make to its peculiar environment. This adjustment is accomplished through education. Bolton makes this clear in his definition of education: "Education is consequently a process of development and of modification or adjustment to environment and to the ideals of perfection conceived by society and by the individual. It involves all the forces operating to mould the individual." [10:11]

Bagley conceived of human adjustment, "the most complicated known type of adjustment," in terms of "social efficiency." The essence of social efficiency was adjustment to prevailing social conditions; it did not imply that the school was to assume leadership in directing social change. The socially efficient person was thus described: "(1) economic efficiency, or ability to pull his own weight' in economic life; (2) negative morality, or the willingness to sacrifice his own desires when their gratification would interfere with the economic efficiency of others; (3) positive morality, or the willingness to sacrifice his own desires when their gratification would *not* contribute, directly or indirectly, to social progress." [3:107-08] That the teacher must understand the need for the submergence of the individual for the benefit of the race was made even more clear. ". . . it is hard to see why the social criterion should not have the

---

[32] For example, Chapter III, "Development and Specialization of the Nervous System and the Significance for Education," and Chapter XIII, "The Nature of Memory Process," are of this type.

position of primacy in a rational theory of education. It is true that the race is composed of individuals, but it is also true that the individual has always been subordinate to the race." [3:110]

That Bolton sensed the importance of the problem of social adjustment is revealed in this statement: "It was originally planned to include a discussion of the sociological phases of education, but the magnitude of the task and the limits and size of the book have prevented." [10:viii][33]

These books would indicate that such interest as there was in the teaching of general educational theory during this period was in no small degree due to the desire to introduce these conceptions from the fields of biology and sociology into the theory of education. It could not be done without considering fundamental principles.

One of the most popular books of the latter part of the period and a book that is still widely used is Chapman and Counts, *Principles of Education* (1924). A more recent book than any of the others described above, it presents a philosophy more in accord with that of the present day, and reflects essentially Dewey's outlook. In its emphasis on education as adjustment, however, it resembles the earlier books, but it differs from them in that it places more emphasis on the dynamic character of society. In urging the theory of adjustment it cautions against thinking of adjustment as mere adaptation to the environment. "The term 'adjustment' as commonly employed may easily carry too narrow a meaning. While in the case of the animal the process may be regarded as consisting essentially of a 'fitting into' the environment, in the case of man, especially in his more advanced types of activity, such a simple statement is apt to be misleading. Adjustment is something more than the forcing of a plastic and passive individual into agreement with a fixed and unchangeable environment." [15:3-4]

Man by changing the environment to suit his needs must play an active part in this adjustment process. "By harnessing the forces of his environment and converting its materials into tools, he is enabled to overcome its more formidable and dangerous aspects. Thus he alters the conditions of life. . . . Any adequate conception of adjustment as a life process must therefore include its twofold

[33] During this period also appeared *Social Principles of Education* by G. H. Betts (1912). The title suggests the social emphasis and the belief that above everything else education should develop "the will and the power to become an active, helpful contributor to the social welfare of the present. Education is therefore a social function and educational values are to be measured in terms of social efficiency." [6:vii.] This in essence was the reason for writing the book.

aspect, involving on the one hand the modification of the organism to meet the external environment, and on the other the modification of the environment to further the ends of life." [15:4]

This belief that man must be an active agent in transforming the environment the better to suit his needs is perhaps the most distinctive feature of the book and constitutes one of its main reasons for advancing general educational theory. This process of changing the environment involved more than making certain physical changes; it pointed directly to the necessity for changing society. The authors' belief that the teacher must understand the social implications of his work and must develop a theory of social welfare is thus stated in the Preface:

Only as a theory of education is guided by such a conception of human values and needs can it hope to fulfill its function in a democratic society. If those who control thought in education and determine its objectives have a sound philosophy, we may confidently assume that an increasing scientific control of the methods of education will help the school towards its true goal. . . . [15:xii]

Quite apart from the contributions of a philosophy of education to professional training, education as a social study must come to occupy a place in the general field of the humanities. Viewed as a mode of social control and as the most powerful force for good or evil in the Great Society, it becomes the most significant, and at the same time the most humanistic, of all the social sciences. [15:xi]

Although it was not stated in bold and convincing terms, the authors shared Dewey's belief that the school should play a leading rôle in the progressive improvement of society. "To a carefully-planned and rigorous system of education, consciously conceived in the light of the need, society must turn, if man is to come into the possession of the skill, knowledge, and character commensurate with his great social responsibility." [15:34]

In thus urging the function of the school in playing the leading rôle in the reconstruction of society and in sensing the maladjustments even at that time becoming more and more apparent, the book anticipated a movement in education which has now taken form. The recognition of the social problem is thus stated: "Is man able to control the forces which he has unloosed on a primitive world? Has he not through his inventions opened a second Pandora's box, more real than the first, out of which have come ills that will eventually work his own destruction? In our economic life there looms a bitter struggle between the different interests engaged in the produc-

tion and the distribution of the fruits of cooperative endeavor."
[15:31]

Even during the period of prosperity when the economic system seemed to be functioning, the authors called into question one of its basic principles—the profit motive. "The existing economic order in its concern for profits has shown such a ruthless disregard for the lives of the workers that in the long run it would undermine its own foundations." [15:258]

More clearly than many other educational leaders of the period the authors understood the meaning of the changes that were taking place in social and economic life and the effects of these changes upon education. After pointing to the transformations wrought by science and invention upon the means of transportation and communication, upon agriculture, industry, and economic and social conditions in general, the question is asked, "How has education been influenced by these economic changes?" The answer was found to be in the widespread inauguration of vocational education on both the secondary and the higher level. Pointing to the inadequacy of such a program in solving the economic problems of the day, the authors urged that "our educational program, therefore, if it is to guard the interests of the entire population and not serve as a bulwark of privilege, must recognize the distribution of income as equal in importance to production itself. The central function of the economic order is that of distributing food, clothing, shelter, and some of the luxuries to all members of society."

This emphasis on the social function of education was quite at variance with the science of education which at that time was approaching the crest of its power and influence. This interest, as has been shown, tended to enlarge the place given the technical courses at the expense of the theoretical courses. That some educators felt the tendency had gone too far is shown in Cubberley's introduction to the book:

"Within recent years, the demand of students in education in colleges and universities has seemed, more than ever before, to be for practical rather than for theoretical courses. This tendency is in keeping with the new demands in other fields of study, and indicates a healthy interest in concrete materials and in training that gives the ability to do. . . . There is danger that those in training today may grow up and pass out of our training institutions without gaining that sound grounding in the philosophy of the educative process which has been the great strength of the older generation of professional educators.

. . . Say all we may in favor of the newer engineering-type of courses of instruction in education, and there is much to be said for them, the fact remains that one of the most important duties of the young teacher or student is gradually to formulate, for himself, a sound working philosophy of the educative process." [15:vii]

This tendency to limit professional preparation for teaching to the "engineering" type of course prompted the authors to write their book on the philosophy of education. They believed teachers should have a broader view of their profession than could be obtained from the technical courses that at that time had become the vogue. "Contrary to the assumption underlying current practice, the growth of our specialized knowledge has made it more rather than less imperative that the student be given a systematic view of the larger rôle played by education. . . . Even though the specialized investigator may scorn philosophy, every investigation reflects some fundamental bias . . ." [15:xi]

Ranking next in importance to the development of the scientific movement during this period is the development of what has been variously called the "Dewey" movement, the "activity" movement, the "progressive education" movement. John Dewey, whose thinking furnished the main source of inspiration for the movement, moved from Chicago University to Columbia University in 1904. Through his teaching and writing he attracted a number of able followers, among whom William H. Kilpatrick and Boyd H. Bode are perhaps the most conspicuous. These men, the former at Teachers College, the latter at Ohio State University, furnished a powerful nucleus for the spread of the movement. Through such books by Bode as *Fundamentals of Education* and *Modern Educational Theories* and books by Kilpatrick as *Foundations of Method, Source Book in the Philosophy of Education*, and *Education for a Changing Civilization*, and through numerous addresses and magazine articles by both men, Dewey's educational theories were interpreted, developed, brought more closely to the problems of the teacher, and more followers were attracted to the movement.

Kilpatrick's teaching at Teachers College, Columbia University, is especially worthy of mention in the part it played in rebuilding the course in philosophy of education. Before he became an instructor at Teachers College, the teaching of educational philosophy had been done by Nicholas Murray Butler and John Angus MacVannel. These men presented the Hegelian outlook which had begun to decline in America. Its metaphysical basis and emphasis seemed unsuited to the American "climate of opinion"; to many it seemed to contribute little toward the solution of current problems. When Kilpatrick was made instructor of philosophy of education the course was commanding only a small following. Convinced that teachers needed the broader outlook which courses in philosophy aimed to give and believing in the value of Dewey's pragmatism, Kilpatrick set about to regenerate the course. Through the use of the discussion method, for which he soon became famous, he attracted large numbers of students to his classes who in turn began to exert a progressively greater influence throughout the country.

Evidence of the spread of Dewey's philosophy is seen in the numerous experimental schools throughout the country and in the widespread use of the language used by Dewey, Bode, and Kilpatrick. One of the earliest experiments in this period to attract national attention was Collings' experiment in the rural schools of Missouri. The Horace Mann and Lincoln Schools of Teachers College have led in the effort to apply Dewey's philosophy to the education of children. Words and phrases used by Dewey, Bode, Kilpatrick are conspicuous in educational periodicals and at educational conventions. Such phrases as "creative education," "activity program," "child-centered school," "activity leading to further activity," "education is growth," have literally become slogans and are frequently used without clear understanding of the underlying philosophy. Rugg said that thousands of teachers pay "lip service" to Dewey's philosophy without having read his basic work. [106: 123 n.] Peterson, in the investigation of which this study is a part, also found that "many are somewhat familiar with its (the Dewey philosophy) terminology; they have learned to speak its language, but, although they may have grasped with considerable understanding its significance with regard to such externals as techniques and devices, they lack an appreciation of its deeper and more far-reaching bearing upon life problems generally." [102:81]

In spite of the apparent popularity of Dewey's philosophy it is difficult to point to much pronounced effect of his philosophic emphasis in teacher-training curricula. As has been shown, professional education continued in the direction of the "practical," the technical and the scientific courses; methods of teaching, psychology, tests and measurements dominated. This was due to the sweep of the scientific movement with its promises of easier educational salvation. It was also due to the exigencies of a frontier situation with rapid increase of population which demanded a large and rapid production of teachers. There was little time to give these teachers the philosophical orientation their work required. The students, too, as might be expected in "practical" America, were looking for "short cuts" to professional competence; they were looking for specific directions and recipes for school teaching.[34]

Perhaps the most significant of Dewey's books that appeared during this period, at least as far as teacher-training institutions are concerned, is his *Democracy and Education* (1916). Its title significantly calls attention to his underlying belief in democracy as the most desirable form of social organization. Dewey believed that the building of a truly democratic society was to a large degree the function of the school, and that it was a matter of first importance that the teacher understand the meaning of democracy. Teachers must realize that democracy meant more than universal suffrage or the public election of government officials. He thus defined democracy: "A society which makes provision for participation in its good of all its members on equal terms and which secures flexible readjustment of its institutions through interaction of the different forms of associated life is in so far democratic." [24:115]

True democracy meant more than physical freedom; it meant intellectual freedom; it meant that the minds of children should not be chained to any set of beliefs. The school in a democratic society must allow freedom for the children to explore and experiment: "Regarding freedom, the important thing to bear in mind is that it designates a mental attitude rather than external unconstraint of movements, but that this quality of mind cannot develop without a fair leeway of movements in exploration, experimentation, application, etc. A society based on custom will utilize individual variations only up to a limit of conformity with usage; uniformity is the chief ideal within each class. . . . A progressive society counts individual variations as precious since it finds in them the means of its own growth. Hence a democratic society must, in consistence with its ideal, allow for intellectual freedom and the play of diverse gifts and interests in its educational measures." [24:357] Again: "Children in school must be allowed freedom . . . to develop active qualities of initiative, independence, and resourcefulness, before the abuses and failures of democracy will disappear." [27:304]

This emphasis on democracy, on freedom in the school, and such other important concepts of the experimentalist philosophy as growth, activity, interest, the instrumental nature of knowledge, the

[34] By interview with John Dewey.

experimental nature of intelligence, the school as the basic agent of social reconstruction, the concept of contingency, of continuity—all meant that the teacher could no longer be limited to set directions of schoolroom procedure. The teacher in Dewey's conception must be guided by broad principles derived experimentally from life. This philosophy, so different from what had previously prevailed, made imperative a reconsideration of theoretical positions; it necessitated intensive study of general educational theory. In the degree that it is held, its very opposition to the more static philosophies which have persisted in our culture will stimulate educators to theoretical activity in their professional schools.

CHAPTER III

PRESENT STATUS OF THE TEACHING OF GENERAL EDUCATIONAL THEORY

SECTION I

THE SOCIAL SITUATION AND EVIDENCE OF REVIVED INTEREST IN GENERAL THEORY

IN 1929 the United States of America suffered a rude awakening. The great physical expansion which had been so characteristic of American history and which the American people seemed to believe would continue without limit suddenly came to an end. The boasted financial system, often referred to as the greatest achievement of American ingenuity, collapsed, ruining millions of people. Many Americans awoke to the realization that the *status quo* philosophy, which in the past dominated the scene, would not work; the old theories of *laissez faire*, of individualism,[1] seemed in a state of obsolesence and the old ideals seemed now only to produce catastrophe. The passion for increasing the production of goods and for creating more and better machines resulted in huge quantities of unsalable goods. The bigger and better idea resulted in monstrous factories filled with idle machinery and in towering skyscrapers filled with vacant rooms. Modern science with its marvelous achievements was of no avail and seemed only to have accentuated the gross maladjustments.

In previous crises of the nineteenth century the vast reserves of land at the command of the federal government served as a correcting mechanism. Those who found themselves maladjusted as a result of a temporary breakdown had an acceptable way for readjustment open to them. Such escape was no longer within the area of possibility. It was no longer possible to evade the problem of political and economic reconstruction by moving to new areas. America was brought face to face with the problem of economic reconstruction as she had never been before.

[1] Dewey phrased it thus: "Rugged individualism had become ragged individualism."

As the depression increased in intensity and its implications bore in on the consciousness of the people, new outlooks and new points of view began to emerge. Gone was the blustering arrogance of the post-Spanish-American War period, gone the exulting complacency of the post-World War period. Instead were to be found deep and penetrating criticisms of the established order. Social observers, philosophers, economists, sociologists attacked the theory of *laissez faire* and the philosophy of individual competition. They criticized the policy of economic nationalism. They called attention to the ever-increasing concentration of wealth in the hands of the few and the tendency for such concentrated wealth to restrict the freedom of the masses. They exposed the reactionary forces of vested interests. They pointed to the miserable housing conditions that prevailed for the millions of laborers and the poorer farmers and to the widespread suffering for lack of food and clothing in a land that was surfeited with commodities of all sorts. Many went so far as to insist that historic capitalism had outlived its usefulness, charging it with the responsibility of wasting the natural resources, of despoiling the lives of millions, and of generating wars. Some openly urged the adoption of methods employed in Russia; some urged the milder methods of Socialism.

Americans began to criticize their political and economic system on a scale never seen before. Symptomatic of the spirit of dissatisfaction with existing conditions, of criticism of the historic institutions, and of the quest for a new way of social living is the vogue enjoyed by such volumes as: *Autobiography of Lincoln Steffens; America's Primer* by Morris Ernst; *Public Pays* by Ernest Gruening; *New Deal* by Stuart Chase; *Decline of American Capitalism* by Lewis Corey; *Method of Freedom* by Walter Lippmann; *Iron, Blood and Profits* by George Seldes; *Robber Barons* by Matthew Josephson; *Choice Before the American* by Norman Thomas; *America Must Choose* by Glenn Frank; *Quest for Security* by I. M. Rubinow; *Technics and Civilization* by Lewis Mumford; *Rebel America* by Lilian Symes and Travers Clement. It is noticed that these books have all appeared since 1930.

The breakdown of the inherited economic and social institutions forced those who were at all capable of thinking to an awareness of the theoretical bases of the accepted ways of conducting the business of society. Social thinkers recognized the formulation of a new theory consonant with modern needs and possibilities as their prime task.

This dissatisfaction with the *status quo* and the revived interest in theory is also reflected in the educational profession. Educators who formerly were chiefly interested in the "science of education" now became social philosophers. Those who in earlier years advocated a reconstructive philosophy of education—educators like Dewey, Bode, Kilpatrick, Counts, and Coe—now urged with increased insistency the necessity of rethinking the educational philosophy of American education.

In the preceding period we have noted that adjustment to the existing industrial order was the underlying idea of education. More than that, industrial procedures made a definite impact on educational practice. Because scientific facts and scientific methods proved of such great industrial value in the advance of industry, educators looked to science as the ultimate oracle in the solution of educational problems. The temper of present-day educational opinion appears to negate many of the beliefs and values held by educators during the Harding-Coolidge-Hoover era. Instead of adjustment to existing industrial conditions, educational thinkers are in search of a method of adjusting industry to the needs of man living in a technological age. That educational systems can be conducted on the same managerial principles functioning in big business is no longer commonly held. Also cast by the wayside is the notion that science alone is sufficient to determine both educational methods and educational aims. In the new temper philosophy is playing an ever-increasing rôle.

The new temper in educational thought is evidenced by the titles of books now enjoying great vogue among professional educators. *The American Road to Culture, Social Foundations of Education,* and *Dare the School Build a New Social Order?* by George S. Counts; *Education for a Changing Civilization* and *Education and the Social Crisis* by W. H. Kilpatrick; *Culture and Education in America* and *The Great Technology* by Harold Rugg; *Education, Crime, and Social Progress* and *Education and Emergent Man* by W. C. Bagley; *Sources of a Science of Education* by John Dewey; *Education for the New Era* by Herman Melville; *Educational Administration as a Social Policy* by Jesse H. Newlon; *The Educational Frontier* by W. H. Kilpatrick (editor), printed as the yearbook of the National Society of College Teachers of Education.

That these authors sense the need for a revision of educational theory in the light of present conditions is revealed in the following quotations. Counts' position is shown as follows:

In a word, the educational and social implications of the machine culture have not been thought through. And until the leaders of educational thought in America go beyond the gathering of educational statistics and the prosecution of scientific inquiry, however valuable and necessary these undertakings may be, and grapple courageously with this task of analysis and synthesis, the system of education will lack direction and the theory of education will reflect the drift of the social order. [78: 193-95]

The American people now find themselves in an economy that is becoming increasingly cooperative and collectivist in nature. As a consequence the magnificent school enterprise, with all of its worship of efficiency and quantitative methods, is harnessed to social purposes that are out of harmony with the facts of the epoch. The more than 5,000,-000 boys and girls now attending the high schools of the country, all looking forward to economic preferment, reveal the bankruptcy of the inherited educational philosophy. The school . . . faces a period of fundamental reconstruction. [79: 282]

Bagley thus urges the need for a revision of educational theory:

The solution in part or in whole, however, will mean a fairly radical revision of many of our educational practices and policies, and the development of a far more virile educational theory than that which has increasingly dominated American education during the past generation. [70: 4-5]

It is the writer's conviction that the ideals which dominate American education today will need a thoroughgoing revision if educational forces are to contribute significantly toward the desired ends. Through no fault of those who have been instrumental in formulating them, our present-day educational theories are, in some ways, actually compounding the already excessive individualism which, in the writer's judgment, is by far the most fundamental factor in the present situation. [70: 13-4]

In 1926 Kilpatrick wrote:

A new philosophy of education is needed: As we face a world changing very rapidly, philosophy, it would seem, must somehow base itself on change or admit its unwillingness to be a force in life's affairs. . . . The new school must be an essentially different school from the old. It will cost more money, not primarily for buildings or equipment, but for the men and women who are to use buildings and equipment. Costly buildings belong to the temper of the present age and on the whole are easily got; but the needed type of officers and teachers is harder to get. It is, however, brains and education and character that we most need and must have. And for getting these a change of philosophy appears to be our only sure hope. . . . Surer even than money to attract men and women of the needed caliber and character is a better philosophy that will free education from its internal thraldom and allow it to do its real work unhampered. Education thus freed and supported can show itself for what it really and truly is—the strategic support and maker of a better civilization. And here, as always, a change of thought must go ahead and show the way. [92:134-36]

Rugg thus called attention to the inadequacy of old theories of education and the need for new ones:

The educational result of this competition of individuals for wealth and power over other men is the American mass school with its mutually inconsistent concepts of conformity to the social group and individual competition for "success." For a century and a half the school was kept apart, untainted by contact with the material civilization of which it is the servant. Throughout our national life the curriculum of the schools has been devoted to passing on descriptions of earlier cultures and to perpetuating dead languages and abstract techniques which were useful to no more than a negligible fraction of our population. Today, therefore, educational reconstruction must confront the task of re-channeling into one broad stream the two isolated currents of practical and cultural life. [107:5]

Dean William F. Russell, in his *Report for the Year Ending June 30, 1930,* said:

What these changes will be no one can predict, but no American school can be called progressive, no demonstration representative of sound educational theory, and no experiment forward-looking, unless there be consideration of the changing world in which we live. We are in great need of economists who can interpret to the schoolmaster the educational needs and demands of this new society of ours. . . .

There is, however, another problem to be considered before we shall arrive at a "sound educational theory." We agree that education should consider the changing world in which we live and that our pupils should be prepared to live in that world. It does not follow, however, that men and women should be content forever to accept the kind of society which we happen to find. . . . We have in the education of the young an instrument by which man may direct his own destiny, a force which if properly applied may be used by society to reshape itself. [152:17-20]

The field of educational administration, which has hitherto been weighted with the minutiae of budgetary accounting, building standards, purchasing procedure, fuel administration, score cards, building maintenance, retirement of teachers, etc., is now beginning to show definite evidence of interest in general educational theory.

School administrators are increasingly coming to the realization that the business management ideal with its accompanying emphasis on administrative techniques which could be easily transferred to the management of delicatessen stores is not adequate for the direction of a school system. In his book, *Educational Administration as a Social Policy* [100], Jesse H. Newlon, himself a school administrator of many years and of national prominence, and a professor of educational administration, condemns the "factual" basis for determining school policies and procedures. He criticizes the tendency to analyze the best existing practices with the object of perfecting the present school system rather than to help create a better system. He expresses himself flatly against the current view of the school administrator as a kind of efficiency expert whose profits take on the form of increased scores on achievement tests. Thus he urges the need for a greater philosophic interest on the part of school administrators: "There has been relatively too much emphasis on the mechanics, on the techniques, on the *how* in a narrow sense, while the deeper social and economic implications, the philosophy and the purposes that should permeate and give direction to administrative procedures have been neglected." [100:101] "Like the study of government, when concerned with forms and methods rather than with substance and ends, it (educational administration) is sterile. Above all else, a social philosophy of school administration is required in the present critical transitional period in American life. [100:252]

Newlon also criticizes the kind of preparation required of administrators. Commenting on a list of topics which was derived from an analysis of eighteen textbooks in educational administration, he says: "It is significant that none of these books attempts to develop a philosophy of education or of educational administration, or inquires more deeply into the larger purpose which administration is designed to serve. . . . There is, of course, a philosophy implicit in these books in their treatment of specific matters; but it is a confused mixture of the prevailing laissez-faire social and economic philosophy and the philosophy of business efficiency, with a vague democracy and Christian idealism." [100:93-4]

He further criticizes the effort to turn educational administration into an exact science. "But the attempt to make of education or educational administration an exact science ignores basic facts concerning the nature and purpose of education and its control. With its attention riveted on techniques developed by application of the methods of the physical sciences to the more obvious and often less difficult problems in the management of the schools, school administration has too frequently failed to sense its major responsibilities." [100 : 264]

There is evidence, too, of a reaction against the earlier faith in the psychological techniques of intelligence and achievement testing. The extravagant promises made by the testers during the second and third decades of the century are now displaced by a tendency to criticize and evaluate these procedures. Goodwin B. Watson, who in the past has made valuable contributions to the testing movement, now evaluates the intelligence test:

How seriously should intelligence-test scores be taken in guiding the life of a child? Does the IQ give a fair and full index of the worth of an individual to society? Most of the harm that has arisen in connection with the use of intelligence tests seems to have grown out of misunderstandings of the answer to these questions. . . .

When the intelligence-test score of an ordinary person is known, that does not tell very much about him. Even in school work, where intelligence would seem to be more useful than anywhere else, the relationship is far from close. Spelling ability is very slightly related to intelligence. Handwriting shows almost no relationship. Exceptions are numerous even in the more "intellectual" subjects. If pupils are grouped by intelligence-test scores into three sections, one bright, one average, and one dull, and if all three sections are given the same reading test, some of the dull section will prove better readers than some of the bright section. If the test be given in arithmetic, in language or science or history, the same result will be found. . . .

Once outside the classroom the significance of an intelligence-test score becomes much more doubtful. Tests in other fields have shown that an individual varies in his abilities. Some things he does well. Others he does poorly. The truth of the matter is that individual intelligence-test scores do not predict any other known ability of the individual with an accuracy that is 50 per cent better than chance. Though we know in general that in the following abilities 1,000 children of high intelligence would excel on the average 1,000 children of low intelligence, we might about as well base our guess as to a particular child's achievement in them on a lottery number, or the length of his big toe, as on his IQ. Personal happiness; popularity with classmates; speed and accuracy of simple learning tasks; mechanical ability; ability to discriminate between good and bad music; ability to sing or play a musical instrument; ability to recognize artistic merit; ability to draw or paint; handwriting speed or quality; cooperativeness, helpfulness; physique, health, athletic ability; persistence; self-control; breadth and variety of play interests; cheerfulness; dependability; speed of decision; self-confidence; ability to keep out of insane asylum during later years, and ability to keep out of prison during later years. This list is not exhaustive. The point, however, may be clear. Whatever may be true about people in large numbers, individual IQ's cannot be taken too seriously. [157]

Similar statements have been made at meetings of the American Psychological Association. At the second spring (1931) meeting of the New York Branch of the American Psychological Association held at Columbia University, *The New York Times* made the following report of an address delivered by Professor Mark A. May of Yale University: "He attacked 'intelligence tests,' asserting that they did not establish the extent of an individual's intelligence, personality, or character, but furnished only samples of his knowledge or 'samples of behavior.' Such tests were of no value except as they furnished statistics, he said." [117]

The New York Times, reporting the 1934 meeting of the American Psychological Association, said: "The emphasis on intelligence tests was attacked by Dr. David Wechsler of Bellevue Psychiatric Hospital, who based his views on practical experience with hundreds of cases. He said it was ridiculous to evaluate a personality through a test of arithmetic, 'remembered' information, or ability to fit patterns together. 'Since the introduction of psychometric tests,' he said, 'psychologists have insisted on identifying mental deficiency with lack of intellectual ability. Medical concepts of mental deficiency, similarly based on single criteria, are equally inadequate when universally applied.' " [116]

In the *Conclusions and Recommendations* of the Report of the Commission on the Social Studies, many of the assumptions on which the testing movement was based were called into question. The following conclusions pertained to intelligence testing:

2. In recent years, owing to the accumulation of evidence of a contrary nature, . . . interpretation of the results of the test has been considerably shaken. At present there seems to be no general agreement among students as to what it is that the test actually measures.

In view of the uncertainty concerning the meaning of intelligence-test scores, the utility of the test in the formulation of social and educational policies is patently limited and is challenged by contemporary social knowledge and thought. [69:90-1]

Achievement testing especially as related to social studies was

severely criticized. Among the recommendations the following are
quoted:

3. The new-type tests, when applied to the social sciences, are subject
to severe limitations: like all forms of schoolroom examination they
are confined to the immediate outcomes of instruction and throw little
if any light on the long time results, but being mechanical in character,
they are even inapplicable to many of the immediate outcomes of instruction.

11. The use by administrative officers of the findings of objective tests
in grading and promoting teachers encourages the latter to concentrate
on the mechanical aspects of learning, thought, and study. When they
form the sole or major basis for judgment they are a menace to education. [69:97-100]

Homogeneous grouping, which as a result of the development of
intelligence testing came to be considered one of the most important educational devices, was seriously called into question by Marvin
Y. Burr and Alice V. Keliher in doctor's dissertations in 1931. [74,
91] Reynolds, of Horace Mann School, Teachers College, thus
states his view of ability grouping:

There followed a period of great activity in intelligence testing. In
a very large number of school systems, group intelligence tests were
given to thousands of children; grouping and school life were determined
almost solely on the basis of this measure. This was the heyday of the
"genius"—the time of the "slow," the "normal" and the "advanced"
classes. The "dumbbell" group came into existence. Educators soon
became aware of the fact that this new panacea for educational ills,
this new formula for solving educational problems, had certain by-
products which were evil. . . .
Within the last decade educators have begun to look upon the education of children from a different angle. . . . In short, some educators
began to see the folly, if not the crime, of completely determining a
child's educational life on the basis of a measurement which, it began
to appear, described, and not too accurately, only a partial segment of
the "whole child"; which measured only one of the many factors that
would contribute to his successful adjustment to life and that should
contribute to his successful school adjustment. . . .
It seems . . . that the intelligence tests as now developed are not
sufficient in themselves to act as a measure by means of which children
in school can be best grouped; indeed, there are few reputable psychologists who would claim this. On the other hand, since the tests do present an easy formula by which this difficult problem of grouping can be
met (not solved), too many school systems are either using them en-

tirely to determine the school life of children or are giving them undue weight in arriving at education decisions concerning children in school. [145]

This shift in educational thought is also evidenced in the content of discussions in periodical literature directed to teachers and in the yearbooks of national organizations of teachers. Twenty-two issues of *School and Society* for the period July through November, 1934, were examined and compared with the same number of issues for a similar period in 1925. This examination was limited to the main articles (usually one or two in each issue) found in the fore part of the magazine. The investigation was guided by the following questions: (1) Is there any attempt to explore the social scene in which education is supposed to operate with the end in view of discovering values to be realized? (2) Does the author recognize the necessity of basic social reconstruction and does he visualize the rôle education is to play in the process? (3) Is there any criticism of the educational philosophy that dominated the school in the past and a corresponding realization of the need for formulating a new philosophy? (4) Is there any attempt to evaluate conventional life values and institutions with a view of developing a more adequate philosophy of life?

The examination of the 1925 issues disclosed practically no discussion of the type suggested by the above questions. The country at that time was prosperous, and educators were chiefly interested in the erection of school buildings, in toying with the new measurement techniques and in the offering of facilities for the increasing enrollments of students. The prevailing discussion is indicated by the following titles: "Responsibilities of Educational Journals for Interpreting the Schools to the Public," "Our Association and Its Work," "Revolutionizing College Environment with Honors System," "Relative Stability of Intelligence Levels," "High School Interest in Methods of Selecting Students for College Admissions," "College Entrance Examination Board." [147]

An examination of the contents of the 1934 issues of *School and Society* reveals that educators continue to discuss the topics that monopolized professional interest in 1926. The remarkable thing, however, is that there is now definite evidence that some discussion centers around the questions indicated above. Note the following titles and quotations here submitted to give some indication of the nature of the articles:

"Traditional Curriculum of the High School Is Challenged by the Activity Program of the Elementary School."

"Prerequisites of Intelligence."

". . . we must admit the need that the college should accept greater responsibility for articulating itself to the rapidly changing conditions of modern life. . . .

"Again, the theory and practice of education must be interpreted very differently according to whether we conceive of life in its long continuity and in its changing aspects or whether we yield simply to its contemporary exigencies."

"Challenge to Education."

"School for the New Social Order."

"It is not less preparation—but more and a different preparation—that our boys and girls need for life in this new social structure. . . .

"The opportunities and responsibilities of the future citizens of our country are greater than they have ever been in the past. The inventions in industry or the 'machine age' have created a situation in social-economic life from which our nation can never return. Life has changed considerably in the last ten years and there is every indication that the change will be more rapid in the years to come. There is no phase of human existence that has not been affected by this evolutionary process."

"Education and Social Change."

"Orientation Courses."

"Will it not present philosophy ready made? . . . fear of indoctrination may be directed against all effective teaching. A man's orientation—does it not amount to his philosophy of life?"

"Work of the Joint Committee on the Emergency in Education for 1935."

"The achievement of genuine educational recovery calls for thought and action in another direction. What is to be the rôle of education in making America a better place in which to live? The troubles of the last four years have served to sharpen understanding of the problems which lie at the root of these difficulties. How are we going to convert an economy of potential abundance into one of actual abundance? How are we going to achieve that modicum of material well-being and security which is essential to cultural and spiritual health? How are we to accomplish sufficient regulation of our common affairs that we can avoid chaos, and achieve stability, and at the same time protect individual initiative and liberty in certain areas? These are the great unsolved questions which confront us who have the privilege of living in this potent twentieth century. . . .

"This situation places a heavy responsibility upon educators of the nation. Logically it is they who should offer the leadership needed in order that schools appropriate to the demands of our times may be developed." [148]

Of the recent yearbooks of the National Society for the Study of Education, only the 1934 issue seems to recognize the need for a new type of education. Earlier yearbooks have apparently been written under the dominance of the notion of "science of education." Since 1904 the only yearbook directed to a discussion of a philosophical nature, with the exception of the 1934 issue, was the famous Twenty-sixth Yearbook, *Foundations and Technique of Curriculum Construction*, which was prepared in 1925. The titles of the yearbooks issued during the four years of the greatest crisis of the American nation do not indicate that education is in the least concerned with the pressing problems of society, nor that society makes any demands upon education. Note the subjects for these four yearbooks:

1930: Report of the Society's Committee on Arithmetic (Parts I and II).

1931: Status of Rural Education (Part I).
The Textbook in American Education (Part II).

1932: A Program for Teaching Science (Part I).
Changes and Experiments in Liberal Arts Education (Part II).

1933: The Teaching of Geography.

It would seem that this organization has been concerned with what may be called schoolroom problems only. It has not been concerned with developing philosophies of education suited to present conditions. It has not recognized the significance of general theory in the formulation of educational programs.

The 1934 Yearbook, however, recognized a movement that had as its aim the more adequate education of children for life in a democratic and changing society—the activity movement. As the subject of Part II of this Yearbook, it includes discussions by some of America's leading educational theorists: John Dewey, B. H. Bode, James F. Hosic, W. C. Bagley, Ross L. Finney, G. B. Watson, W. H. Kilpatrick.

The yearbooks for the American Association of Teachers Colleges were examined to note evidence of interest in general educational theory. Beginning with 1924, the tables of contents were scanned and the title of every third address was recorded. Following is a list of subjects discussed in more than one address:

The organization of teachers colleges.
Standards of normal schools and teachers colleges.
Health programs in teacher-training institutions.
Plans of teacher education in various states.
The preparation of instructors for teacher-training institutions.
Teachers college curricula.
Training school facilities.
Financial support.
Regulating supply of teachers.
Placement service.

The above list of subjects fairly represents the interests of the American Association of Teachers Colleges, as expressed in their yearbooks for the past ten years. Here, too, the chief concern seems to have been with surface problems and with educational techniques. In the sampling only one address was found that suggested the need for reconstruction of theory. This address is entitled, "Education for a New World," and was delivered by Jesse H. Newlon.

The same technique was employed in the examination of the yearbooks of the National Society of College Teachers of Education. The following subjects were mentioned more than once:

Supervision.
Administration of intelligence tests.
Selection of teachers for the public schools.
Improvement of methods of teaching professional courses.
Research in education.
Curriculum problems (of teacher-training institutions).
Predicting success in college by means of tests.
Problems of liberal arts colleges.
Practices of American universities in granting higher degrees (Subject of yearbook—No. 19).
The direct contributions of educational psychology to teacher training. (Subject of yearbook—No. 20).

The 1933 Yearbook was, however, of a radically different nature and it has gained a considerable hearing among educators under the title *The Educational Frontier.* A group of educators who for some time have identified themselves with problems of educational theory prepared the most complete and comprehensive treatise on the philosophy of education that has appeared in the past decade. The following chapter headings reveal in a measure the nature of the book:

The keynote of the book is set forth in the following paragraph:

It is in this need for reconstruction that we find the new educational frontier. At present educators are insensitive to this need, in direct proportion to their pretensions of scientific impeccability or to their sentimental absorption in the development of the individual child. A new emphasis is necessary if the scientific method in education and the concept of individuality are to become meaningful. It is necessary if education is to make its proper contribution toward safeguarding the future. [93:31]

The emergence of a new educational magazine, *The Social Frontier*, under the editorship of George S. Counts, in the fall of 1934, is further evidence of revived interest in general educational theory. Carrying the subtitle, "A Journal of Educational Criticism and Reconstruction," its purpose is essentially to present a new theory of education. This new theory is needed, according to its editorial staff and board of directors (who are among America's leading educational philosophers), because civilization is passing through a transition from individualism to collectivism. From this assumption it follows that an education adapted to meet the needs of an individualistic society must be transformed if it is to meet the needs of a collectivistic society. Such transformation calls for a reconstruction of educational theory. In the first issue this journal editorially states its purpose:

The Social Frontier assumes that the age of individualism in economy is closing and that an age marked by close integration of social life and by collective planning and control is opening. For weal or woe it accepts as irrevocable this deliverance of the historical process. It intends to go forward to meet the new age and to proceed as rationally as possible to the realization of all possibilities for the enrichment and refinement of human life. . . . Also it proposes, in the light of this great humanist principle (the Declaration of Independence) applied to the collective realities of industrial civilization, to pass every important educational event, institution, theory, and program under critical review. Finally, it will devote its pages positively to the development of the thought of all who are interested in making education discharge its full responsibility in the present age of social transition. Its editorial staff and board of directors hope that it will help fight the great educational battles—practical and theoretical—which are already looming above the horizon. And they trust that it will engage in the battles of the twentieth and not the eighteenth century. [150]

SECTION II

STATUS OF GENERAL EDUCATIONAL THEORY IN TEACHER-TRAINING INSTITUTIONS

We have now passed in review certain conditions affecting the teaching of general educational theory. The economic depression which crashed upon the American people in 1929 stimulated interest in social, political, and economic theory. It stimulated interest in educational theory. While some areas in professional education still reveal little interest in philosophical problems, other areas show considerable activity. This we noted in certain educational books, in the magazine *School and Society*, in the emergence of a new magazine, *The Social Frontier*, in the yearbooks of certain national organizations. We noted also a definite skepticism of the business management type of education offered prospective school administrators and of the techniques developed by the intelligence testers. In other words, there are some areas in American education where the *status quo* is questioned—where there is an active quest for a philosophy of education adequate to meet the exigencies of present life. Among some leaders in education problems of educational theory seem to be the most pressing problems of education; they seem to feel that if the American people are to move forward to a richer life, a reconstructed philosophy of education must operate in the public schools.

To what extent do teachers' training programs of the past few years reflect the growing recognition on the part of educational leaders that it is only through a reconstructed philosophy of education that education can function in the reshaping of American life? With the end in view of finding an approximate answer to this question, the writer has examined material bearing on: (1) the relative extent to which courses in general theory are prescribed in teacher-training institutions as compared with the degree of prescriptions in the previous periods; (2) the emphasis placed on theory by those majoring in education—this emphasis being measured by the number of courses in general theory of education pursued as compared with the total number of courses taken; (3) the opinion of teachers in education as to the importance of the contribution made by general theory courses to the professional preparation of teachers; (4) the topics discussed in courses entitled Introduction to Education, Principles of Teaching, and Principles or Philosophy of Education. The cumulative evidence of the material examined seems to point to a considerable lag of teacher-training programs and opinions of the rank and file teachers in institutions engaged in professional training of teachers behind the program that seems to be implied in the discussion of educational leaders.

On the basis of Deyoe's study [82:75] it appears that the tendency to curtail theoretical courses in education in the teacher-training curricula noted in our discussion of the previous period continues unabated in the period intervening between 1922 and 1932. Philosophy or principles of education dropped in the two-year curricula from 20 per cent in 1922 to 3 per cent in 1932. During the thirty-year period, 1902-1932, the drop was from 27 per cent to 3 per cent. Likewise is the decline in the number of institutions requiring history of education noticeable. In 1922, 29 per cent of the institutions offering two years of normal work required history of education, in 1932 only 6 per cent; in 1902 history of education was a required subject in 89 per cent of the institutions.

In contrast with this drop in the theoretical subjects the technical and scientific courses continued or even improved their positions. As in 1922, so in 1932 observation and practice were required in all the institutions studied. There was, indeed, a slight drop in general and educational psychology from 100 per cent to 97 per cent, and in psychology of the elementary school subjects from 5 per cent to 3 per cent; but in the case of genetic psychology there was an increase of 20 per cent to 28 per cent. Tests and measurements remained at the 1922 level of being required in 22 per cent of the institutions studied. The tendency toward greater emphasis on specialized courses is evidenced by the introduction into the required list of two new courses not included in the required list in 1922. Administration and rural education are required in 6 per cent of the schools.

Similar trends are noted by Deyoe in the four-year curricula. [82:76] Philosophy or principles of education required in 1922 in 30 per cent of the institutions was required in 1932 in 27 per cent. The decline in history of education was from 52 per cent to 47 per cent. Again in contrast with the indicated decline in theoretical courses, it appears that "scientific" and specialized courses at least maintained their position; indeed, general and educational psychology dropped to a slight degree from 100 per cent to 97 per cent; psychology of the high school subjects from 22 per cent to 13 per cent, and administration and supervision from 15 to 10 per cent; but on the other hand, genetic psychology, including the psychology of adolescence and childhood, showed an increase in prescription from 13 to 23 per cent; principles of secondary education, from 39 to 60 per cent. The most marked rise in importance of any single subject is noted in the case of tests and measurements required in 1922 in 26 per cent of the four-year curricula, but included in the prescribed list of 50 per cent of the institutions in 1932. The consistently high percentages of prescribed courses in the technical fields suggest the conclusion that in American teacher-training institutions education is still an applied science.

Class [76:42] listed all the subjects required by at least 50 per cent of thirty-four state teachers colleges "in their two-year, three-year, and four-year courses" for all levels of teaching for which students are prepared; that is, kindergarten, grades one and two, grade three, junior high school, rural schools, etc. The course, principles or philosophy of education, which most purely represents educational theory does not appear in any of the curricula nor for any of the levels of teaching. On the other hand, child psychology is required in 56 per cent of the kindergarten curricula; "curriculum" in 60 per cent of the kindergarten and grades 1 to 3, three-year curricula; educational measurements ranges from 50 per cent to 83 per cent; educational psychology is required in more than 50 per cent of all the curricula and for all the levels of instruction with the range being from 60 per cent to 100 per cent, with a mode of above 80. Required to almost an equal extent is general psychology.

Class's list includes courses in which presumably some attention is given to theoretical problems. Thus history of education is required in 50 per cent of the four-year junior high school curricula; general method and principles of teaching are required in most of the curricula and for most levels of teaching, the requirement ranging from 54 to 89 per cent of the institutions; and introduction to education is required in about two-thirds of the curricula for the various levels with a range of between 50 and 67 per cent. It should be noted, however, that these courses do not have as their major objective the advancing of general educational theory.

In an exhaustive study of the history of professional education for teachers, Frazier makes the following summary statement which corroborates the findings reported above and indicates the tendency towards narrow, highly specialized courses:

Educational psychology is now probably the most frequently taught among the professional courses; and closely related courses, such as child study and tests and measurements, are common. General psychology, usually taught as a subject preparatory to educational psychology, still ranks high. History of education has changed considerably in nature and no longer occupies its previous high place in order of frequency. Courses in school administration and school supervision have been broken up somewhat into specialized courses under different titles. School management, principles of education, and principles of teaching, introduction to education or to teaching, educational philosophy, special methods courses in considerable variety, rural education, educational sociology, and the curriculum are among the other professional courses in modern teachers college and normal school curricula. Courses have become greatly specialized, particularly in large institutions; and there is much confusion in terminology and a great deal of overlapping among courses. [83]

Even those who major in education select a higher proportion of their courses from the technical and specialized groups. This becomes clear from the supplementary report of curricula in teacher-training colleges and normal schools prepared by Earl U. Rugg of the National Survey of the Education of Teachers. [106:51] Rugg lists twenty-eight courses in education taken by education majors graduating from teachers colleges and normal schools, indicating the per cent of the total number of students who have taken a particular course, and the average median of credits earned by the group. For the purpose of determining the importance attached to general theory courses by students majoring in education, the present writer has selected from the mass of Rugg's data those bearing on philosophy of education, history of education, educational sociology on the one hand, and those bearing on educational psychology, tests and measurements, and curriculum on the other. The first group of courses may be considered as falling within the category of general theory of education, though this is not quite so clear in the case of educational sociology. The second group may be considered as falling mainly within the scientific-technical courses.

Of the more theoretical courses philosophy of education was taken by 37 per cent of the four-year majors with an average median of 2.6 credits, and 7 per cent of the two-year majors with an average median of 3.8 credits. History of education was taken by 65 per cent of the four-year students majoring in education with an average median of 2.9 credits. Educational sociology was taken by 22 per cent of the four-year majors with an average median of 2.7 credits, and 10 per cent of the two-year majors with an average median of 2.6 credits.

On the other hand, relatively much higher percentages of students majoring in education took technical or scientific courses and for a larger number of credit hours. Educational psychology was taken by 91 per cent of the four-year majors in education with an average median of 6.5 credits, and 67 per cent of the two-year majors with an average median of 3.5 credits. Tests and measurements was taken by 65 per cent of the four-year majors with an average median of 3 credits, and 42 per cent of the two-year majors with an average median of 2.2 credits. Curriculum was taken by 54 per cent of the four-year majors with an average median of 4 credits, and 17 per cent of the two-year majors with an average median of 2.8 credits.

For the purpose of discovering the value attributed by teachers to general theory courses in the professional preparation of teachers, the writer has undertaken a study of twenty-five teachers colleges, normal schools, and liberal arts colleges.[2] For this study parts of the questionnaire and instrument mentioned in the first chapter were used. Full description of these devices is not necessary at this point. Suffice it to say that the questionnaire included a number of items formulated for the purpose of directly eliciting teacher opinions of the value of courses in general educational theory. The instrument, consisting of seventy-nine propositions dealing with educational issues to which teachers were asked to register agreement or disagreement, contained six propositions phrased to compel the respondent to give his approval or disapproval of general theory courses. Of the 511 individuals who responded to this investigation, 56 were instructors of general theory courses; namely, philosophy or principles of education, theory of teaching, principles of teaching, introduction to education, technique of teaching, history of education,

[2] The location of the institutions is given on page 7.

integration courses and some types of courses in educational sociology. The instrument was also given to a group of professors at Teachers College whose combined scores are used only for purposes of comparison. In the ensuing pages reference will be made to those items of the questionnaire and propositions in the instrument pertinent to the present problem of discovering the opinions of the instructors regarding courses in general educational theory.

It is believed that six propositions, all bearing on the same point should give, with reasonable accuracy, the opinions of instructors concerning this phase of professional education. [102:IV] Proposition 9 of the instrument reads as follows:

9. The place given to specific techniques and measurements in the professional education of teachers today should be reduced rather than increased.

On this proposition the votes stood: non-theory teachers, 37 per cent in favor of an increase in techniques and measurements rather than a decrease; theory teachers, 49 per cent; and the group of professors at Teachers College 24 per cent. It is impossible to say whether this increase should take place at the expense of general theory or subject-matter courses. However, it is a reflection of a view that the education of teachers is somewhat like the education of an engineer—an applied science—or is somewhat like a skilled trade learned by placing emphasis upon techniques. It is surprising that theory teachers themselves cast the highest vote in favor of increasing technical courses.

The proposition next in order bearing on general theory is:

31. A course in general educational theory can be as close to the vital and immediate needs of the prospective teacher as is the provision for his technical training and supervised practice.

On this proposition the votes were: non-theory teachers, 45 per cent against general theory; theory teachers, 22 per cent; professors, 16 per cent. Almost half of the non-theory teacher vote registered the belief that technical training and supervised practice were of greater value than instruction in general theory courses. Even one-fifth of the theory teacher vote expressed the same view.

The next proposition regarding general theory reads as follows:

36. The need for courses in general educational theory in teacher-training institutions should gradually disappear as a growing science of education shall continually improve our techniques and objective tests and measures.

On this proposition the votes were: non-theory teachers, 37 per cent in favor of the belief that a science of education would eventually displace general theory courses; theory teachers, 16 per cent; and professors, 10 per cent. More than one-third of the non-theory teacher vote seemed to reflect a view that with the growing techniques of scientific investigation for discovering the facts, there would be no need for theorizing or philosophizing on education. From this vote one might assume that the voters regarded theorizing as a kind of elaborate guessing, and the teaching of theory courses as an indication that education is still in a primitive state. These courses represent in the minds of many a transitory state in the development of education towards an exact science.

The proposition next in order bearing on general theory is:

44. Seeing that "natural philosophy" has been superseded by the exact sciences, we may expect that philosophy of education will be eventually superseded by the science of education.

Forty per cent of the non-theory vote, 30 per cent of the theory vote, and·6 per cent of the professor vote expressed the belief that "philosophy of education will eventually be superseded by the science of education." This proposition presents essentially the same idea as proposition 36 above. They represent the extreme scientific view.

The proposition next in order bearing on general theory is:

45. General theory frequently fails to become operative in the teacher's practice because it is by nature so abstract as to prove functionally effective for only a few of the gifted students.

This proposition revealed a widespread lack of faith in the efficacy of general theory courses. Seventy-four per cent of the non-theory teacher vote, 56 per cent of the theory teacher vote, and 44 per cent of the professor vote agreed that general educational theory "is by nature so abstract as to prove functionally effective for only a few of the gifted students." It is noted that the votes against theory are much higher for each of the groups than for any of the other propositions. This vote is a clear indication that many believe general theory is so abstruse and far removed from the problems of teachers that for the rank and file it is of little value. It is an indication of the common belief that theory is separate from practice. Is this analogous to comments often heard about the so-called "brain trust"—"Practical men are needed in Washington, not theorists?" An examination of the relationship of theory and practice will be found in Chapter V.

The last proposition bearing on general theory is:

49. For the prospective teacher to have a good course in general principles of education and no specific training, would be better than for him to have only the technical and specific training and no course in general principles of education. (Supposing he could have only one or the other, not both.)

This proposition states the case very clearly. The issue is brought out in the open as to whether courses in principles of education or technical or specific courses are thought of as possessing more value in the education of teachers. The votes are 56 per cent for the non-theory teachers, 39 per cent for the theory teachers, and 28 per cent for the group of professors. It is perceived that more than half of the non-theory teachers and more than one-third of the theory teachers favor technical and specific courses as against the study of principles of education.

In order to broaden the scope and check upon the data explained, the instrument of seventy-nine propositions was presented to instructors in the National Survey of the Education of Teachers. The returns of more than 2,000 instructors were available for comparison. This should give a fairly good index of the nation as a whole. Table I was prepared to compare the votes of the National Survey

TABLE I

PERCENTAGE OF VOTES CAST AGAINST GENERAL THEORY IN SIX
PROPOSITIONS OF INSTRUMENT BY ALL GROUPS

Proposition	National Survey	Non-Theory Teachers	Theory Teachers	Professors
9. Techniques and measurements to be increased	45%	37%	49%	24%
31. Technical training and practice more valuable	54	45	22	16
36. Science of education will displace theory	39	37	16	10
44. Science will supersede philosophy of education	44	40	30	6
45. Theory too abstract for average student	73	74	56	44
49. Technique and specific training alone more valuable	54	56	36	28
Average score	52	48	35	21

with those of the groups discussed above. The table also contains a summary of the votes on the six propositions.

It is noticed at once that there is a surprisingly close agreement between the scores made in the National Survey and those made by the non-theory teachers. This suggests that the study made by the writer of the twenty-five institutions is fairly representative of the nation. Fifty-two per cent of the National Survey votes and 48 per cent of the non-theory group votes were in opposition to theory.

The proposition that drew the highest vote in opposition to theory was No. 44, which stated that theory was too abstract to be of use except for "only a few of the gifted students." Seventy-three per cent of the votes of the National Survey group and 74 per cent of the votes of the non-theory group expressed this view. This means that throughout the teacher-training institutions of the country approximately three-fourths of the instructors believe theory of little value for the average student. The theory teachers concurred with a vote of 56 per cent. It is very significant that more than half of the teachers of general theory believe that their material is of value for only a few of the gifted students.

As one might expect, the theory teachers cast fewer votes in opposition to theory. But even here we are surprised to find that 35 per cent of their total vote was against the teaching of general educational theory. The professors consistently were less opposed to theory than any other group.

The questionnaire included four items bearing on the opinions of the instructors concerning courses in general educational theory, among which was the following:

9. Indicate with a check your opinion of courses in general educational theory (as now taught):
   ( ) Of practically no value in the preparation of teachers.
   ( ) Of some value, but not worth the time spent.
   ( ) Of great value.
   ( ) Indispensable in a teacher-training program.

Of the 460 non-theory teachers who responded to this question, 6, or 1 per cent of them, said courses in general educational theory are of practically no value in the preparation of teachers; 182, or 40 per cent, said, "Of some value but not worth the time spent." These two statements are interpreted as expressing essentially low regard for courses in general educational theory. The responses taken together number 188, or 41 per cent of the total number of non-theory teachers who express disfavor of the value of general theory courses as now taught. One hundred and twenty-eight, or 28 per cent, said, "Of great value"; and 144, or 31 per cent of the total, said, "Indispensable in a teacher-training program." These latter two statements express approval of the general courses and their total responses equal 272, or 59 per cent of the total.

The theory teachers, as might be expected, are more in favor of the general courses, but they do not by any means express 100 per cent agreement as to their value. None checked the first item, but ten of the fifty-five persons in the theory group who responded said, "Of some value but not worth the time spent." For some reason these instructors are uncertain of the very material they teach. A partial explanation may be found in the fact that seven out of the ten theory teachers who so reacted are not full-time teachers of general theory courses. There is evidence that the practice of giving general theory courses to instructors who also teach other courses is fairly common. Twenty-four theory teachers, or 44 per cent, indicated that they believed theory courses are of "great value," and twenty-one, or 38 per cent, reported "indispensable." The reactions of both groups of Item 9 indicate that approximately one-fourth of the theory teachers and somewhat less than one-half of the non-theory teachers express disapproval and serious doubt as to the value of courses in general educational theory as they know them.

Since a considerable proportion of those engaged in teaching education and even theory of education believe that courses in general educational theory are of little or no value, the considerations which enter in the teacher's estimates of general theory courses are of decided interest. A question asking the instructors to give reasons for their attitude toward the general courses was incorporated in the questionnaire. The question reads as follows: "State one or two important reasons for your reaction to No. 9 above." The answers were classified as to whether they were favorable or unfavorable to the teaching of general theory. The unfavorable responses are given in Table II.

It is seen at once that the most frequent objection to courses in general theory on the part of the non-theory teachers is that they are "too abstract and theoretical." It reflects the common view that theory and practice are two different things and that one is useful and the other is not. It reflects the view that what teachers need is not theory but something "practical"—that is, courses in methods, subject matter, or practice teaching. In any consideration

TABLE II

REASONS FOR NOT FAVORING COURSES IN GENERAL EDUCATION THEORY

Reason	Non-Theory Teachers	Theory Teachers
1. Too abstract and theoretical—too general	80	5
2. Too much separation from practice	73	8
3. Too much repetition in general theory courses	51	5
4. Poorly taught—teachers lack experience	43	3
5. Subject-matter courses more valuable	37	2
6. Courses poorly organized—ground too thin	13	2
7. Too much time devoted to these courses	13	—
8. Fail to interest students—trivialities—no challenge to intellect	9	—
9. Professionalized subject matter better	8	—
10. Too many methods courses*	8	1
11. Common sense and experience better	4	—
12. Theory courses consist largely of meaningless jargon	4	1
13. Courses promote too many fads and experiments	3	—
14. Too many conflicting views in education	3	—
15. Courses too highly standardized	2	—
16. Classes too large	2	—
17. Too much emphasis upon textbook	1	—
18. Vast amount of worthless reading	—	1

* General theory courses undoubtedly confused with methods courses.

of the function of theory, this objection must be considered. A discussion of theory and practice will be found in Chapter V.

The next most important objection was "too much separation from practice." This objection is essentially the same as the one discussed above in that theory is thought of as separate from practice. However, there is another factor that may have entered into this objection. Some may have made the statement not because they believe theory and practice are inherently separate, but because the instructors of these courses fail to establish an organic relationship between them. In other words, it may in some cases be a protest against the way these courses are taught rather than an indictment of the teaching of theory as such. However, the high vote for both items 1 and 2 leads to the conclusion that the relation of theory and practice is a serious question. It is significant that eight out of the fifty-six theory teachers expressed this objection to their own courses.

The third most frequently mentioned objection is "too much repetition." This is a common criticism of general theory courses and it has been substantiated by many studies. [133, 122, 131] This is not so much a criticism of theory as theory, but rather a criticism of the teaching of theory. It suggests the necessity of defining more clearly the content of the general courses.

The fourth item in point of frequency is "poorly taught." Some added "teachers lack experience." It is difficult to determine whether this comment means lack of practical public school experience on the part of theory teachers or lack of experience in teaching theory. At any rate it is criticism of the way these courses are taught. Such frequent objection to theory courses because of the manner of teaching them points to the necessity of examining the fitness of theory teachers for their work.

Among other objections to theory courses is the belief that "subject matter courses" are more valuable. Apparently the belief persists that if teachers only know their subjects thoroughly they can teach well without theory. Another objection, "common sense and experience better than theory," is suggestive of the argument of the backwoods farmer against "book larnin'." Some seem to think that success in teaching depends not upon studying the theory of education, but upon rolling up one's sleeves, using "common sense," and "lighting into the job." There were other criticisms of theory courses, such as "courses poorly organized"—"too thin ground," "fail to interest teachers—deal in trivialities," "theory courses consist largely of meaningless jargon." As has already been suggested, it is likely that the instructors of the theory courses are themselves to blame, in part, for the unpopularity of these courses.

The considerations that led the instructors to ascribe value to theory courses are given in Table III.

Of the reasons for favoring theory, the one mentioned most frequently was "underlying laws and principles of education and teaching." There is reason to believe from the context of some of these statements that some respondents meant principles of teaching rather than the broader principles of education. On the other hand, some intended to express their approval of the teaching of the general principles of education. The phrase "underlying laws" suggests the views expressed by nineteenth century textbook writers that education was based on "certain immutable laws and principles."

The reason for favoring the teaching of theory next in order of frequency is "give perspective and background." It resembles item No. 6 (broader view of education) in that it suggests the belief that teachers need a broad point of view the better to perform their

TABLE III

Reasons for Favoring Courses in General Educational Theory

Reason	Non-Theory Teachers	Theory Teachers
1. Underlying laws and principles of education and teaching	62	5
2. Give perspective and background	43	3
3. Training in methods necessary to teaching	42	7
4. Orientation and integration	30	8
5. Philosophy of education	22	6
6. Broader view of education	18	3
7. Results of teaching prove their worth	16	3
8. Students and teachers like these courses—help them to achieve self-confidence	15	1
9. Help students to profit by experience of others	12	1
10. Necessary to get psychological approach	8	1
11. Necessary to develop thinking	8	2
12. Application of knowledge to teaching	8	4
13. New viewpoints	5	0
14. Trends of education	4	1
15. Evaluation of theories	4	1
16. Meaning of education	3	0
17. Acquire educational vernacular	3	0
18. Inspiration	2	0
19. Develop professional attitude	2	4
20. Professional ethics	2	0
21. Personality development	2	0
22. Valuable because developed by experts	2	0
23. General culture	2	1
24. Sociological approach	2	1
25. Vocational guidance	1	1
26. Supply laboratory experience	1	1
27. Aid teacher in maintaining discipline	1	1

task. This meaning constitutes a laudable reason for favoring general theory. In fact, the development of a broad point of view is here held to be the chief function of courses in general educational theory; it will be given more extended treatment in Chapter V.

The third reason for favoring general theory courses is "training in methods necessary for teaching." This represented a complete misunderstanding of the function of general theory courses. Their function is not to teach methods. This statement is an indication of the passion for technical courses which has been so characteristic of faculties of teacher-training institutions.

Thirty individuals thought courses in general educational theory should serve the function of "orientation and integration." These are popular words among educators and undoubtedly they are sometimes used without adequate understanding of their meaning. Do they mean that courses in general educational theory help the student to formulate a clear conception of the meaning of education, give him direction in his work, help him to see the various aspects of education in their mutual relationships, the various disciplines in the light of the contributions they should make to the education of children, and the place of education in contemporary society? If this is what is meant by "orient and integrate," the words point to a most important factor in the education of teachers.

It is interesting to note some of the other considerations that operate in the favoring of general theory, such as "aid the teacher in maintaining discipline," "necessary to get psychological approach," "vocational guidance," etc. As will later be discussed, these are not directly the functions of general theory courses.

Further information on the status of general educational theory is furnished by the replies to question No. 11 of the questionnaire.

11. Rank the following courses in the order of what seems to you to be their value for prospective teachers. (Use numerals 1, 2, 3, etc. for first, second, third, etc.)
    ( ) Educational sociology
    ( ) Philosophy of education
    ( ) Introduction to teaching
    ( ) Principles of teaching
    ( ) History of education
    ( ) Principles of education
    ( ) Technique of teaching

Responses to this question were made by simply marking a "1" opposite the course of first choice, a "2" opposite the course of second choice, and so on. These numerical rankings were totaled in two groups—the theory group and the non-theory group. According to the method used, the course receiving the lowest total would rank first, in the opinions of the respondents, the one next lowest, second, etc. Table IV gives the rankings.

Of these general courses in education it is seen that the more "practical" courses—practical in the sense of dealing with matters pertaining directly to school procedures, such as principles of teaching, introduction to education, technique of teaching, are most highly evaluated, while the more purely theoretical courses and the courses

TABLE IV

RANKINGS OF PREFERENCES OF COURSES IN GENERAL EDUCATIONAL THEORY
OF 25 NORMAL SCHOOLS, TEACHERS COLLEGES AND LIBERAL ARTS COLLEGES
CLASSIFIED IN TWO GROUPS, THEORY AND NON-THEORY TEACHERS

Theory	Educ. Soc.	Phil. of Ed.	Introd. to Ed.	Prin. of Teach.	Hist. of Ed.	Prin. of Ed.	Tech. of Teach.
Theory Teachers...	6	5	1	2	7	3	4
Non-theory Teachers........	6	5	2	1	7	4	3

emphasizing the social aspects of education, history of education, educational sociology, philosophy of education, are rated near the bottom. These courses have all suffered from the movement to make professional education "practical." The theory teachers agreed with the non-theory teachers that history of education, educational sociology, and philosophy of education are of least value for prospective teachers.

The questionnaire contained one further item relative to the opinions of instructors as to the rôle of general theory courses in the education of teachers:

Do you believe that general educational theory should be taught in separate courses or that it should be taught in connection with the subject-matter courses?

This question was asked because some educators have urged the curtailment of courses in general education. The view has been advanced that most of the theory should be taught in connection with subject-matter courses. Of the 438 responses of non-theory teachers to this question, 236, or slightly more than one-half (54 per cent), favor the teaching of general educational theory in subject-matter courses, and 202, or 46 per cent, favor separate courses. Certain qualifying statements on some of the questionnaires indicated a feeling that, essentially, educational theory should be taught with subject-matter courses, but that there should be a separate "introductory" course.

Among the theory teachers, as might be expected, there are more individuals favoring separate courses for the teaching of general educational theory. Thirty-eight of the fifty-six theory teachers, or 70 per cent, so expressed themselves. But even among the individuals who teach these courses, 30 per cent prefer the teaching of general theory with professionalized content courses. (Of these, eight indicated theory should be taught both in separate courses and in subject matter.)

These data seem to corroborate the other findings of the study relative to the opinions of the instructors regarding courses in general educational theory. Except for the theory teachers, one-half favor the combining of theory with subject-matter courses as against the separate courses. Apparently the general theory of education is not of sufficient importance to merit specialized study. The reactions to the six propositions in the instrument made by the 551 individuals included in this study and the 2,000 included in the National Survey indicate that approximately 50 per cent of the instructors do not approve of the teaching of general theory. Similarly, the responses to the four questions in the questionnaire indicate that a high valuation is not placed on the treatment of the broadly theoretical aspects of education, but, rather, opinion favors the treatment of matters more narrowly practical.

In the foregoing pages, evidence was presented to show that general theory courses do not occupy an important place in the programs drawn up for the professional education of teachers, and that, moreover, their importance is continually declining; that even students majoring in education take relatively little work in the philosophic aspects of education; and finally that a large proportion of teachers believe general theory courses are either superfluous or of little value. To get a complete picture of the status of general theory courses in teacher-training programs, it is necessary to examine the content of the courses themselves.

A detailed examination of the material of the general courses— the textbooks and the syllabi used—would manifestly be impossible. Some information bearing on this question was obtained by examining Kruse's study of principles of teaching, MacDonald's [137] study of the content of introduction to education, together with several textbooks used for this course, and by making an analysis of the descriptions of principles or philosophy of education found in sixty 1932 catalogues divided equally among normal schools and teachers colleges, liberal arts colleges, and departments of education at state universities.

As has been pointed out, the course in principles or technique of teaching is considered in this study because it usually includes some material of a broadly theoretical nature. The main purpose of the course, however, is to deal with "problems of stimulating and directing the learning activity of pupils under school conditions. It deals with teaching activity as distinct from learning activity, which is the subject matter of educational psychology." [95:146]

From an examination of the 1927-1928 catalogues of twenty-five institutions, Kruse prepared a table of topics mentioned more than once. [95:95] From this list of twenty-one items some were noted that suggest the type of material included in our definition of general educational theory. There is no certainty that these topics always included consideration of the basic philosophy involved; they were selected because they suggest the possibility of such discussion.

"Principles or theory of teaching" was mentioned as a topic in eleven of the twenty-five catalogues examined. It is included here because in the degree the discussion of this topic seeks to base educational theory and practice upon life purposes and needs, in the degree it seeks to expand the student's conception of the meaning of education, it is properly philosophic in nature and comes within the category of general educational theory.

"Interest and motivation" was also mentioned in eleven of the twenty-five catalogues. This topic is suggestive of both the Herbartian and the Dewey philosophies of education. It is included here because theories of interest and motivation are rooted in conceptions of the nature of the individual. Study of the topic ought to help the prospective teacher see the task of education in relation to life needs and interests and as such should broaden his conception of education.

"Aims and objectives" was mentioned in only nine of the twenty-five catalogues, but judging from the frequency of mention in textbooks used in this course [95:100] the treatment of the topic is more general than the above number would indicate. Any discussion of education in terms of aims and objectives is philosophical in the degree that these aims are related to life. Such a discussion should open up for the student the broader aspects of education, showing, for instance, how the school is an agency for helping the individual live the best life of which he is capable and an agency for the continuous remaking of society. Of course, this topic may, and often does, mean nothing more than the memorization of one, five, seven (or whatever the number may be) "aims of education," which "aims" are recited in class and reported in examinations, and as such make little contribution to the expansion of point of view. The extent to which this is done is not known, and no conclusions can be made. But the topic is essentially philosophic.

"Project method" was mentioned nine times. It suggests Kilpatrick's theory of school procedure and is commonly associated with Dewey's educational philosophy. It is based on certain conceptions of the nature of the individual, of the nature of interest, and often of the social nature of education. In the course "principles of teaching," it is probable that more attention is devoted to the technique of the project method than to the underlying philosophy. In the degree the course considers the theories on which the project method is based, it comes within the category of general educational theory.

"Selection of subject matter" mentioned in five catalogues may involve consideration of the philosophy of education upon which such selection should be based, or it may consist merely of memorizing the various methods of "curriculum building" without consideration of the theory involved. It may represent an effort to apply the techniques of activity analysis. As such, the topic would take on the character of educational science and educational techniques rather than general educational theory.

"Moral education," mentioned in three catalogues, suggests consideration of general principles of conduct; it suggests the consideration of life values. Any effort to study life values is philosophical [142] and is properly to be thought of as general educational theory.

These six topics have been described to show how principles of teaching may to some extent be a course in general educational theory, but they do not bulk large in the course. The other twenty-four topics of the list are more closely related to that function of the course of which the following are typical: drill and practice, lesson planning, supervised study, use of standard tests.

The same conclusion is borne out by Kruse's analysis of chapter headings found in seventeen textbooks on principles of teaching. Of the forty main groups of topics, only seven would seem to involve discussion of a broadly theoretical nature. These seven group headings are here listed together with the number of chapters found under each.

1. Motivation (14 chapters)
2. Stimulating thinking (14)
3. Aims of education (9)
4. Function of education (8)
5. Moral, social training (6)
6. Selection of subject matter (5)
7. Principle of self-activity (4) [95:100]

As to the vogue enjoyed by this course, Kruse concluded that most teachers colleges offer a course of this type whether it be called principles of teaching, technique of teaching, or general method. In institutions of two-year curricula he reported that of 116 teachers colleges and normal schools examined, one-half of them required it. [95:148]

The course "Introduction to Education" as usually given touches upon subjects which legitimately fall within the category of general educational theory. This course emerged when the development of a great number of specialized courses made the need for an introductory orienting course increasingly clear. [14:2] Among the earliest educators to see the need for such an orienting introductory course are Thorndike, Bagley, and Cubberley. Bagley first offered an introductory course in 1908; in 1913 he used the title, "Introduction to Education," and Thorndike's *Education; a First Book* as a text.[3]

Because of the belief that education was rooted in the recently developed scientific psychology, the introductory course was thought of largely in terms of introduction to psychology and the principles of teaching based on it. Thorndike gave as his purpose in writing *Education* the preparation of students "to see the significance of their more specialized studies in educational psychology and sociology, methods of teaching and class management, the history of educational theory and practice, and the applications of philosophy and ethics to education." [64:v] Similarly, others who developed the course gave large place to psychology. This is shown by the recommendations for an introductory course in education made by the Missouri Survey of teacher-training institutions. More than any other thing, this report gave impetus to the new course. [76:43]

The survey recommended the offering of a course which "should furnish a bird's eye view of the teacher's task, and . . . might well be termed an Introduction to Teaching rather than an introduction to psychology." The psychological emphasis is revealed by this description: "Aside from an initial effort to define in simple and concrete terms the problem of teaching, it would be largely psychological in its character, very concrete and 'practical' in its content, and concerned with such topics as instincts, habits, the laws of learning, the technique of study, and the significance of individual differences—topics that have a definite application to classroom teaching." [96:182]

[3] By interview.

An examination of several of the early textbooks shows that psychology of the teaching process remained central for some time. [4, 40, 30] Later writers, however, used history of education as the central theme. The historical approach was made by Cubberley in his *Introduction to the Study of Education and Teaching* and by Clapp, Chase, and Merriman in their text, *Introduction to Education*. Even in these books, however, a large place is given to the psychology of learning and to discussions of principles of teaching. As the course developed, it came to include such other topics as management and administration of schools, the social relations of the school—play and recreation, parent-teacher associations, the school as a community center—methods of teaching, the American public school system, teaching as a vocation, personal qualifications of the teacher.

In addition to the above topics, it is significant that most of these books include a chapter or two on problems of general educational theory under such headings as "aims of education," "function of education," "philosophy of education." These chapters are broadly theoretical in that they endeavor to clarify the meaning of education and to make more clear to the student the function of the school. Sometimes this is done chiefly through a discussion of other educational philosophies, as in Cubberley's book; sometimes through a discussion of various aims of education, such as happiness, utility, service, morality, as in Thorndike's text.

The contents of this course were made a subject of study in 1930 by MacDonald. [137] In response to a questionnaire containing a check list of topics sent to ninety-six institutions in thirty-eight states, it was revealed that the topics teaching as a profession and teacher relationships received the most emphasis. Psychological aspects of teaching, techniques of teaching, educational administration, discussions of the main fields of teaching (nursery, kindergarten, elementary), and historical aspects of education were emphasized by more than half of those responding to the questionnaire.

In the list of topics in the check list, only one suggests general educational theory—aims of education. But for the purposes we have in mind the check list was hardly adequate. Aims were listed only under the various specialized fields—nursery, elementary, kindergarten, etc., which would lead one to believe that only aims for specialized fields are considered in the course. Whether general or specific, however, the majority of those responding indicated that aims of education were emphasized.

An examination of some of the more recent textbooks indicates that theoretical material is considered in the course more than might be suggested by MacDonald's study. A growing realization of the importance of developing in this course a conception of education adequate to meet the needs of present-day society is present. Blackhurst's *Introducing Education* [7] includes a chapter on "Meaning of Education," one on "Sociology in Relation to Education," one on "Meaning of the School Curriculum." Still more emphasis on general educational theory is found in Adams and Taylor, *Introduction to Education and the Teaching Process,* where one whole section, Part V, is devoted to "Philosophy of Education."

More recent than any of the books mentioned above is Burton's *Introduction to Education.* One section treats of "Function and Aims of Education," including chapters on "Education," "Society and the Individual," "The Aims of Formal Education," "Discussion of the Value of Education." Part II, "Method of Educational Thinking," is a discussion of the rival claims of science and philosophy.

Deyoe's study [82:75-6] shows that this course has become exceedingly popular in teacher-training institutions. In 1902 it was required in only 2 per cent of the institutions offering two-year curricula; in 1922, 9 per cent; but by 1932, 69 per cent. In the four-year curricula the course does not appear until 1922, when it is required in 9 per cent of the institutions; by 1932 it is required in 63 per cent of the schools.

Analysis of catalogue descriptions of principles or philosophy of education of the sixty teachers[4] colleges and normal schools, the liberal arts colleges, and the departments of education at state universities yielded the topics listed in Table V.

The great number and variety of topics is noted at once. Forty-six different topics were found of which twenty-three were mentioned only once; the topic of greatest frequency was mentioned seventeen times. Judging from this list, what conclusions can we formulate on the contents of principles or philosophy of education?

[4] An effort was made to secure a random sampling of these catalogues as follows: in the stacks the catalogues of the normal schools and teachers colleges were arranged alphabetically according to the state in which the institution was located. The first 1932 catalogue of alternating states was selected until twenty catalogues had been obtained. The liberal arts colleges were arranged alphabetically according to the names of the institutions. The first catalogue for 1932 of alternating letters of the alphabet was selected, until the number 20 was reached. The state universities were arranged alphabetically according to state. The first 1932 catalogue of alternating letters was selected.

TABLE V

TOPICS FOUND IN DESCRIPTIONS OF PRINCIPLES OR PHILOSOPHY OF EDUCATION IN 60 CATALOGUES DIVIDED EQUALLY AMONG NORMAL SCHOOLS AND TEACHERS COLLEGES, LIBERAL ARTS COLLEGES, AND DEPARTMENTS OF EDUCATION IN STATE UNIVERSITIES FOR THE YEAR 1932–1933*

Topic	Normal Schools and Teachers Colleges	Liberal Arts	Depts. of Education	Total
Aims of education	4	6	7	17
Integration	8	2	5	15
Evolution of trends	4	2	3	9
?Curriculum	1	6	2	9
Develop a philosophy of education	—	3	5	8
Social function of education	3	3	1	7
*Methods	4	2	—	6
*Psychology of learning	2	2	1	5
Criticism of curriculum and proposed educational theory	1	—	4	5
Give a philosophy of life	2	2	—	4
Education a life process	—	—	3	3
Democracy and education	1	1	1	3
*Organization, administration or management of school	—	1	2	3
Education and the individual	2	—	1	3
Problem or foundations of method	—	1	2	3
Doctrine of interest	—	1	1	2
Purposeful activity	—	1	1	2
*Extra-curricular activities	—	2	—	2
*Types of education	1	—	1	2
Solution of present-day problems	2	—	—	2
?Educating agencies	—	1	1	2
Changing conceptions of education	—	1	1	2
Forces reconstructing school system	2	—	—	2
*Arouse and organize professional view	—	—	1	1
Education and philosophy	1	—	—	1
?Seven cardinal principles	1	—	—	1
*Familiarize with names of education	1	—	—	—
Education as adjustment	1	—	—	1
Education as growth	1	—	—	1
Implications of education—religious	—	1	—	1
Implications of education—ethical	—	1	—	1
Implications of education—economic	—	1	—	1
Freedom and authority in a democracy	1	—	—	1
School as an institution in society	1	—	—	1
?Principles underlying practice	—	1	—	1
*Application of principles	—	—	1	1

TABLE V (*Continued*)

Topic	Normal Schools and Teachers Colleges	Liberal Arts	Depts. of Education	Total
*Selection and training of teachers	—	—	I	I
*School activities	—	—	I	I
*Support of education	I	—		I
Process of thinking	—	—		I
Coercion	—	—	I	I
Professional ethics	—	—	I	I
*Correlation of studies	—	I	—	I
*Lesson plans	—	I	—	I
*Conduct of recitation	—	I	—	I
?Improve existing educational practice	—	—	I.	I
Total				139

* Topics that seem irrelevant to principles or philosophy of education are marked with an asterisk. Doubtful topics are marked with a question mark.

In scrutinizing the list it is necessary to remember that topics that suggest the expansion of point of view, the criticism of ideas, notions, and theories of education, the relating of the school to social and life needs properly come within the scope of general educational theory. Topics were looked for which indicate the weighing of life values, the developing of a working point of view for dealing with the many conflicting demands of life. Any effort thus to clarify the nature of the good life, or the good society should define the problem of education and give direction to the work of the teacher. Of these forty-six topics, twenty-eight seem to fit in with this conception of general educational theory, of which only seven were mentioned more than three times.

"Aims of education" was mentioned most frequently. This is also a favorite topic in principles of teaching and introduction to education, and as pointed out in the discussions of these two courses should allow considerable discussion of a philosophical nature. However, if aims are not criticized and evaluated, but presented dogmatically, to be memorized, the course, so far as developing the viewpoints of the students is concerned, can be of little value. "Integration" was mentioned in fifteen, or exactly one-quarter of the sixty catalogues examined. This word is used so loosely that it is difficult to make any appraisal of the appropriateness of this topic in principles or philosophy of education. If the word is used for the type of treatment that does not stop with the mere collecting of information from the various aspects of professional education and from the various academic subjects, but goes on to help develop in the student a unified and consistent outlook on life and education, it is properly philosophical in nature.

"Evolution of trends" may involve a discussion of the evolution of educational theory and as such should help expand conceptions of education. The discussion of this topic, in so far as it makes clear the developing conceptions of education in relation to the development of civilization, showing the close relation between educational aims and practices and the social patterns of various stages of development; in so far as it helps the prospective teacher relate his work to the needs of the individual and of society by leading him to reflect upon what historic educational thinkers have written, is broadly theoretical. In the sense that evolution of trends means historical facts to be memorized, it is not so considered.

The topic "curriculum" appeared nine times. It is also included in principles of teaching and was appraised in the discussion of that course.

The fifth topic in order of frequency is "develop a philosophy of education." Obviously, this topic is most appropriate in a course in principles or philosophy of education and no comment should be necessary. Obviously appropriate, also, is the topic, "social function of education." The other topics which suggest the possibility of philosophical treatment were mentioned but five times or less.

Some of these topics reveal the influence of the Dewey-Kilpatrick philosophy, such as "education a life process," "democracy and education," "purposeful activity," "doctrine of interest," "problem of method." This evidence of the experimentalist philosophy in the course principles or philosophy of education may seem to contradict the conclusion that the Dewey school of thought has not greatly affected teacher-training curricula. Previous discussion tended to show that the force of the scientific movement reduced teacher-training curricula largely to courses in science of education and techniques of education. The actual course offerings seem to be dictated by educational science, not Dewey's philosophy; but that is not to say that in the general theory courses themselves the Dewey emphasis is not to be found.

This list of topics also shows that there is no clear conception of the function of principles or philosophy of education. It shows that too often the course has abandoned its philosophic functions and attempts to treat subjects that properly belong to other courses. "Methods," for example, ranked seventh in the list and the "psychology of learning" eighth. It appears from this that not only have the techniques and scientific courses gained the dominant position in the professional curricula but the spirit and subject matter of these courses have also invaded the very courses intended to develop a philosophic insight of education. A scanning of the list of topics marked with an asterisk reveals such other non-philosophical subjects as psychology, school management, extra-curricular activities, educational administration, etc.

There is evidence that the course "principles of education" has frequently become a kind of "catch all" for various topics in education that may have been slighted in other courses. For example, a certain workbook for Principles of Education includes such varied topics as: aims of education, the nature of teaching and learning, support and control of American public schools, educational tests, statistics, how to get a position. [50] Bruce, in 1931, wrote that principles of education was a conglomeration of materials including some psychology, history of education, sociology, "a chapter about biological bases, frequent reference to specific methods old and new, criticism of curriculum construction, measurement movement, touch of ethics, and perhaps a little philosophy." [125] He characterized the course as "boarding house hash."

Scrutiny of these topics shows little realization of the social crisis through which civilization is now passing or that principles of education is in any way involved. There is little suggestion of the needs of life today.[5] "Solution of present-day problems," twice mentioned, suggests the clearest recognition of social problems. The topic "social function of education" ranking sixth, although mentioned only seven times in all the sixty catalogues, also suggests a recognition of social problems. Judging from other phrases used in the catalogue descriptions and the manner of treatment in most textbooks, however, we may consider the "social function of education" to mean that it is the function of the school to adjust itself to present-day conditions. The school is viewed as an agency for adjusting individuals to the existing economic and social order rather than as an agency for assisting in the direction of social change.

It is also quite obvious that the course is still chiefly concerned with the development of the individual. Such topics as "psychology of learning," "education and the individual," "doctrine of interest,"

---

[5] The failure to draw the subject matter for this course from the present social scene is shown in the reference to the use of such a textbook as Ruediger's *Principles of Education* published in 1910.

"education as adjustment," suggest this emphasis. The conclusion seems warranted that at a time when society seems to be changing from an individualistic to a coöperative basis general educational theory courses are still preparing teachers for an individualistic society. There seems to be no recognition of the fact that more and more society is shifting to a coöperative basis and that the chief function of the public schools is to prepare children for this new society.

The writer is aware of the limitations of a catalogue study in that course descriptions are frequently so much "window dressing." But such descriptions often do represent what the instructor thinks *ought* to be done, and in general it is believed an honest effort is made accurately to describe these courses by mentioning the most important topics. It would be erroneous, therefore, to assume that failure to mention topics of a philosophical nature means that the courses do not actually deal with philosophical problems or that when philosophical topics are mentioned a genuinely philosophical discussion is always implied. But with all these allowances, it seems fair to conclude that, in general, courses in principles or philosophy of education are not properly devoted to a consideration of the general theory of education and are disappointingly unaware of current social problems.

CHAPTER IV

QUALIFICATIONS AND PHILOSOPHIES OF TEACHERS OF THEORY COURSES

SECTION I

QUALIFICATIONS OF TEACHERS OF GENERAL THEORY

WHAT can be known about the persons who are teaching courses in general educational theory in the schools of this study? Are they professionally trained for the work they are doing? Is their experience such as to qualify them for teaching such courses? What is the nature of their intellectual interests as revealed by their reading? What can be learned of their social philosophies? How do they stand on certain crucial issues in educational theory and practice? It is the purpose of this chapter to look into the preparation of teachers of general educational theory, their fitness for such teaching, the nature of their reading interests, and their social and educational philosophies.

TABLE VI

DEGREES HELD BY 56 TEACHERS OF GENERAL EDUCATIONAL THEORY

Degree	Number	Degree	Number
Ph.D.	13	B. A.	3
Pd.D.	1	B. S.	5
M. A.	26	B. E.	1
M. S.	1	Normal school diploma	4
M. Ed.	1	Nothing reported	1

Of the fifty-six theory teachers who responded to the questionnaire thirty-nine were men and seventeen were women. The median age of the men was 46, with a range from 26 to 68; of the women, 36, with a range from 29 to 65. Some idea as to the academic preparation of the group can be gathered from Table VI, giving distribution by degrees held or diplomas received.

It thus appears that thirteen teachers of theory, or 23 per cent of the group studied, hold the Doctor's degree; forty-two, or 77 per cent, have an academic preparation equivalent or superior to that represented by a Master's degree; nine, or 15 per cent, report the Bachelor's degree; and five, or 9 per cent, fall, as far as formal education is concerned, below the college equivalent of a Bachelor's degree. It is noted that fourteen, or 25 per cent, report no graduate degree, although all but one of these report attendance at summer schools within the past five years.

It is extremely hazardous to pronounce these paper qualifications "good," "poor," or "fair." For purposes of comparison it might be helpful to submit some figures concerning the training of teachers in other phases of higher education, such as the liberal arts college. Data are here submitted which were gathered in a questionnaire study of 163 institutions in the North Central Association. Of the 8,743 faculty members who responded, 33.9 per cent held the Ph.D. degree or its equivalent; 7.5 per cent had two years of graduate work; 33.8 per cent the M.A. degree; 22.3 per cent the B.A. degree, and only 2.5 per cent less than the four years' undergraduate training. [144] By including the group having two years of graduate study with the M.A.'s to correspond with data gathered in this study, the total percentage for the M.A.'s is 41. A comparison of the liberal arts faculties and theory teachers can be made from the figures in Table VII.

TABLE VII

COMPARISON IN PERCENTAGES OF DEGREES HELD BY THEORY
TEACHERS AND TEACHERS IN LIBERAL ARTS COLLEGES
OF NORTH CENTRAL ASSOCIATION

Degree	Theory Teachers	Liberal Arts Teachers
Doctor's	25%	33.9%
Master's	50	41.3
Bachelor's	16	22.3
No degree	9	2.5

It is seen that the liberal arts group has a higher percentage of individuals with the Ph.D. and the B.A. degrees and the theory teachers a higher percentage of individuals with the M.A. degree and with no degree of any kind. On the whole, the average is somewhat lower for the theory teachers than the liberal arts teachers, and this in spite of the fact that the liberal arts faculties often include graduate students who teach. Although there is no criterion by which to judge, it would seem that the theory teachers should at least be as well trained as the liberal arts teachers. This is not to imply that an advanced degree is a guarantee of superior performance. It has frequently been charged that in American education too much reliance is placed upon degrees—that there exists a kind of "degree worship"; that individuals with high degrees are chosen for positions of great responsibility regardless of such other factors as character and personality; that salaries are gauged and graduated according to the degree held, with the result that many teachers are being stampeded into a mad rush for high degrees. It can hardly be doubted that there is truth in each of these charges.

None the less the fact remains that until better methods for gauging a teacher's preparation are discovered, the possession of a degree may be used for whatever merit it has as a measure of professional equipment. By and large, it must be admitted that a group of Ph.D.'s would be likely to be more thoroughly oriented in the field of their major study than a similar number of Bachelors.

With the end in view of discovering the "alertness" of the theory teachers to the need of continuing growth and development, data on summer school and extension course attendance were secured. Here too, it is recognized as altogether possible that a person may take extension courses and attend summer schools and yet achieve little intellectual development, and that on the other hand many individuals achieve intellectual and professional attainments without the benefit of the summer session or the extension course. Yet for the group as a whole, figures as to attendance on courses would most probably constitute an index of intellectual and professional alertness. The investigation has revealed that thirty-seven individuals, or 66 per cent of the entire group, attended a total of sixty-four summer sessions in the course of the past five years, and that nineteen, or 33 per cent of the total, attended fifty-two extension courses during the same period. Probably most of this work represents efforts toward a higher degree. These data do not afford a basis for determining the degree of alertness of the theory teachers inasmuch as no facts for a comparable group are offered. It is, however, not unsafe to assume some positive correlation of the theory teachers with the whole group in this respect.

Do instructors in educational theory possess an adequate preparation for teaching in this field? No definition of what constitutes adequate preparation has been here undertaken. It is apparent, however, that in most cases teachers who have not majored in educational theory are not likely to possess an acquaintance with the subject matter and problems of educational theory sufficient to teach in the field. Teachers of educational theory were asked the question: "Major subject in graduate school?" "In undergraduate school?" A summary of their responses is tabulated herewith. (Table VIII.)

TABLE VIII

FIELDS OF MAJOR STUDY IN GRADUATE AND UNDERGRADUATE SCHOOL

Graduate Major		*Undergraduate Major*	
Education	18	Education	11
Educational administration	8	Social science	12
Educational psychology	3	Languages (including 3 for Latin)	6
Secondary education	3	Science	6
Teacher training	3	Mathematics	3
Education and other subjects	2	Philosophy	2
Educational supervision	2	English	2
Sociology	2	Liberal arts	2
Normal school administration	2	Agriculture	1
Elementary supervision	1	Rural education	1
Latin education	1	Elementary supervision	1
College administration	1	Law	1
Rural education	1		
Geography	1		
English and education	1		

It is noticed that eighteen persons, or 32 per cent, majored in "education" in graduate school and eleven, or 20 per cent, in undergraduate school. Because of the looseness of the term "education" it is difficult to determine what this means. It is conceivable that a number of those majoring in education have taken considerable work in educational theory. Just how many, cannot be ascertained on the basis of the returns. In many institutions education is used as a generic term to include all courses relating to the profession of teaching and as such includes courses in psychology, administration, general and special methods, educational measurements, educational theory, etc. A major in education could be one of a great many things. An indefinite number of those who reported as having majored in education probably had some preparation for the teaching of theory courses. However that may be, the other 68 per cent of the group majored in the various specialized fields of educational administration, psychology, college administration, and even the sub-ject-matter fields of geography, English, and Latin. From these data the conclusion may be drawn that the large majority of the group are inadequately prepared for the teaching of educational theory.

To ascertain more fully the extent of preparation of these teachers in the field of general educational theory a further question was ad-dressed to them:

7. What courses in general educational theory have you studied? (This is meant to include any course which, in your judgment, put primary stress upon educational theory. The following titles sug-gest the type of course meant: philosophy of education, principles of education, theory of teaching, principles of teaching, introduc-tion to teaching, technique of teaching, history of education, integra-tion courses; and some types of courses in educational sociology, etc.)

From the responses to these questions it is learned that four teachers have had only two courses in general educational theory and five only three courses. In other words, 16 per cent of the present group have had three courses or fewer in the field in which they are teaching. For the remaining forty-five instructors four or five courses in general educational theory is the average.

Cook [77] set up standards for preparation in subject specializa-tion. He considered twenty-four semester hours of undergraduate work in the subject a person is teaching, and fifteen hours of grad-uate work—a total of thirty-nine hours—as necessary to equip one properly. By considering the theory courses to have been given an average of three hours a week,[1] a means for comparison is avail-able. In these terms, four theory teachers have had six hours in the field they are teaching, five had had nine hours, and forty-five an average of between twelve and fifteen hours. As compared with the amount of special preparation recommended by Cook, the con-clusion seems warranted that these instructors have not properly recognized general theory as a field of specialized study.

It will be observed that with the exception of three who in the course of their graduate studies majored in subject-matter fields, all have majored in one or another field of education. This, how-ever, should not be interpreted as mitigating the inadequacy of the preparation of the group for the teaching of educational theory.

[1] An examination of school catalogues reveals that there are more two-hour general courses than four-hour. Occasionally a one-hour course was listed.

Next in size to the group having a graduate major in "education" is the group that reported having a major in administration. This course has become so technical and specialized that it could hardly be considered pertinent to the teaching of general educational theory. In fact, it has often prided itself in the definiteness and specificity with which it attacks the problems of school administration. It has been concerned primarily with preparation for the duties of the school superintendent involving such matters as finance, business accounting, school building programs, pupil accounting, relations with national, state and local authorities, school publicity, public relations, personnel management, etc.

In the same way, the other specialized fields, such as educational psychology, secondary education, are definitely concerned with the more technical problems of their respective interests. They do not aim to provide the general and more inclusive approach of general educational theory. And it might be added that a person with such specialized training as is furnished by one of these fields is likely to teach the general course from the biases and narrower interests of the specialized study. As will be explained in Chapter V, such preparation can scarcely be considered adequate to accomplish the purposes of general educational theory.

In indicating that teachers of educational theory are inadequately prepared for their task, it is by no means desired to suggest that such teachers be subjected to a narrow discipline of specialization in educational theory. It is fully recognized that no one is qualified to teach the broader aspects of education without an acquaintance with a number of the professionalized specialized fields. However, anyone who teaches theory should have at least as much preparation in educational philosophy, history of education, and other courses which rise above immediate procedures and techniques for the purpose of exploring the considerations which necessarily must be taken into account if education is to function significantly in life, as the school administrator, the school psychologist, and the supervisor have in their respective fields.

It would thus seem that anything like adequate specialized training for the teaching of general educational theory is utterly lacking. The teaching personnel for these courses is made up of individuals who have specialized in other subjects, or phases of education, who "took" a few general courses along with their major subject (either because of certification requirements or because they wished to do so) and who are now "given" these courses to teach.

On the assumption that public school experience is an important element in the qualifications of teachers of general theory the following question was asked:

8. What teaching experience have you had? (including administration)
   Institution   Subjects or grades   Title of position   No. of years

The responses indicate that theory teachers as a group have had considerable public school experience both elementary and secondary. Only two persons report no public school experience, and but one instructor only one year of elementary experience. For the rest, fifteen report only secondary experience and nineteen only elementary school experience. It would, perhaps, be granted that both elementary and secondary experience are, however, equally valuable as preparation for the teaching of general educational theory.

Added to the inadequacy of preparation for the teaching of general educational theory, it would appear that the administrative arrangements of teacher-training institutions are such as to assign the task of teaching general theory to persons unprepared or not especially interested in doing so. This will be evident from the answers to the following questions given by the individuals in the group studied.

1. What is your present teaching program?
2. What was your teaching program last semester (term)?
3. What school duties other than teaching do you have? (Administration, supervision, coaching, teacher placement, etc.)
   (a) In terms of class hours per week, about how much time do these duties require?

From the responses it appears that many teachers of general educational theory have other duties, such as supervision, practice teaching, acting as dean of women, or teaching of subject-matter courses. Out of the fifty-six teachers of theory courses, forty-four report other duties. Six individuals report work of from 1 to 4 hours per week in addition to the teaching of theoretical courses, eight, from 4 to 8 hours, and thirty, more than 8 hours per week.

The reasons for the large number of instances where teachers of general educational theory are required in addition to engage in other fields of education are numerous. It is difficult to account for every particular instance. The two major reasons, however, seem to be (1) "farming out" of courses in general educational theory to persons whose interests and preparation lie in quite different fields. Probably such practice flows from the assumption that educational theory is not a specialized field and consequently any member of the faculty is thought capable of teaching it. (2) The desire on the part of theory teachers to engage in some educational activity which might give concrete content to theoretical concepts and considerations.

To state, therefore, that general theory courses are "farmed out" in every case where other subjects and extra duties are reported would be quite inaccurate. An effort was made to determine as accurately as possible the number of cases where the evidence seemed to show that individuals were teaching these courses more because of administrative expediency and necessity than because they were specifically trained.

Where other class and extra-class duties were reported, the questionnaires were carefully scrutinized for additional pertinent evidence. Such points were noted as: present position, title of extension courses studied, major subject in graduate and undergraduate school, the number of theory courses studied as a student, the nature of past school experience, the amount and nature of duties other than teaching theory. On these bases, it appeared that in approximately one-third of the cases the courses in educational theory were "farmed out." This judgment is of course in the nature of an estimate; it is manifestly impossible to arrive at an exact figure. But great care was taken to include only those cases where the evidence of "farming out" did seem convincing. Doubtful cases were not included.

To indicate more clearly what is meant when it is alleged that a course is "farmed out," a number of sample cases are reported:

Case No. 20. Present position—Dean of Women.

Degree held—M. A. Extension courses—none. Major subject in graduate school—Latin and education. Major subject in undergraduate school—Latin and education.

Courses in theory of education studied—introduction to teaching, school management, history of education; mention also made (although not asked for in this question) of courses in measurements, deanship, and three courses in methods of teaching Latin.

Experience—3 years, high school principal and teacher of Latin. 1 year, dean of women and teacher of Latin in college. 2 years, Latin and English in a college. 1 year, dean of women and Latin in college. 2 years, dean of women, Latin and education.

Present teaching program—6 hours, deanship of women. 3 hours, Latin. 3 hours, educational sociology or history of education.

School duties other than teaching—extracurricular activities and dean of women.

It is not contended here that this person is incapable of teaching the two courses involving educational theory. It might be that her experience has been so organized as to make her theory courses most valuable. But there seems to be conclusive evidence that her chief interest is not general educational theory, but Latin and deanship. Nor could it be claimed that she had any special preparation for the teaching of general theory courses. Had a like amount of time and effort been expended in preparation for the teaching of chemistry or history as was here used in preparation for the teaching of educational theory, it is improbable that the person would have been considered qualified to teach such courses. Many people believe that "anyone can run a farm," and apparently the same conviction is held with regard to the teaching of general theory courses in teacher-training institutions.

Four more cases are submitted:

Case No. 93. Present position—instructor.

Degree held—A. B. Extension courses—Have taken one or two courses every year for last 6 years on Saturday at Columbia and N.Y.U. in education. Major subject in graduate school—school administration. Major subject in undergraduate school—mathematics and philosophy.

Courses in general educational theory studied—educational sociology, experimental education, determination of policy, history of education.

Experience—3 years grade teacher. 7 years elementary school principal. 3 years supervising principal. 1 year teacher of education.

Present teaching program—4 hours, introduction to teaching. 3 hours, educational measurements.

School duties other than teaching—teacher placement, supervision of practice teaching—15 hours.

Case No. 266. Present position—director of training.

Degree held—none specified. Extension courses—none. Major subject in graduate school—education. Major subject in undergraduate school—jurisprudence.

Courses in general educational theory studied—37 semester hours in administration, philosophy, psychology, history of education.

Experience—3 years, rural school. 5 years, director of athletics and pedagogy. 21 years, director of training.

Present teaching program—3 hours, psychology. 3 hours, sociology.

Other school duties—director ot training—80 per cent of time.

Case No. 92. Present position—instructor and dean of women.

Degree held—A.B. Extension courses—major course for advisers of women—philosophy of education, study of religions, contemporary education. Major subject in graduate school—none given. Major subject in undergraduate school—Latin and German.

Theory courses studied—introduction to history of education, philosophy of education (perhaps same as mentioned above) : "Do not recall college courses in sufficient detail to give accurate information." Experience—2 years rural school. 4 years high school teacher and preceptress—German, English, algebra. 10 years, normal school teacher and critic and supervisor, dean of women. 4½ years, assistant to principal in public high school, followed by a university position—English and school management.

Present teaching program—5 hours, principles of education. 4 hours, home economics. Same for second semester except that problems of teaching substituted for principles of education.

Other duties—dean of women, selection of critic teachers, from 7 or 8 to 12 or 15 hours per week.

Case No. 467. Present position—principal of training school.

Degree held—A.M. Extension courses—none. Major subject in graduate school—educational administration. Major subject in undergraduate school—sociology.

Courses in general theory studied—principles of education, history of education.

Experience—2 years elementary school teacher. 5½ years high school teacher of science, mathematics, Latin. 7 years, head of department of education in normal school, teacher of child psychology, introduction to teaching nature study.

Present teaching program—3 hours, introduction to teaching. 20 hours per week, general supervision of the school.

These cases illustrate a condition that seems to be fairly common in American institutions for the education of teachers, namely, that many present teachers of general educational theory have not specialized[2] for that type of work, but are teaching one or two of these courses in addition to other duties which are more directly in line with their major interests. For such persons, theory courses are essentially a "side line." This may help to account for the fact that theory courses are in disrepute. When general educational theory does not represent the major interest of those teaching it, and does

---

[2] "Specialized" study does not here mean a narrow, exclusive attention to restricted aspects of education. Since education involves all of life, "specialized" study here means an intensive investigation into as many of the more fundamental and significant problems as possible, and as such involves a thoroughgoing consideration of the history, philosophy, and sociology of education from the critical point of view.

not command their most sincere efforts, it is to be expected that aliveness and vitality will frequently be lacking.[3]

Another effort to get a picture of the teaching personnel of theory courses was made by inquiring into the type of reading done. Three questions were used:

13. Name two educational magazines that you find most helpful in your work as teacher.
14. Name not more than three general magazines that help you most in understanding current social movements and events.
15. Give the titles of what you consider the five most significant books (of any kind) you have read in the past three years.

It is reasonable to assume that in answering these questions some of the teachers reported not so much what they actually did as what they thought they should have done. This tendency to give oneself the benefit of the doubt, and thus report oneself in a better light than the actual situation would warrant can be assumed to have been a factor in some of the results obtained. Mention was probably made of magazines read infrequently, and books known only remotely or thought should be read. In some cases where part of a book was read, or even reviews of it, it may be assumed that the temptation to include it among those read was yielded to. If nothing else, it can be claimed that the magazines and books mentioned represent the kind of reading that it is felt *ought* to be done, and perhaps, is likely to be done when more favorable opportunities are present. In other words, this situation is not worse than the actual facts.

Following are the frequencies of mentions of educational magazines reported to have been found helpful by those who have responded:

School and Society	18
Educational Administration and Supervision	16
N. E. A. Journal	15*
Elementary School Journal	9
Journal of Educational Research	8

[3] After these cases had been selected, their scores were ascertained on the "instrument" and on Harper's A Social Study. The scores are such as to bear out the original conviction that the courses are, in these cases, "farmed out." On the instrument the votes are: 78–82; 35–95; 56–76; 98–83; 72–78; or, in other words, practically a 50–50 vote, indicating great inconsistency, and lack of thorough orientation in educational problems. For further description of meaning of votes on the instrument, see pages 139 f.

On Harper's the scores were: 64, 56, 69, 65, 47. Only one person is above the median for this type of group. The rest are below, extending as low as 47. For further explanation of the Harper instrument, see pages 137 f.

Teachers College Record   8
Progressive Education   6
Journal of Educational Psychology   5
School Review   3
Educational Method   3
The Psychological Review   3
American School Board Journal   2
Junior and Senior High School Clearing House   2
Nation's Schools   2

American Journal of Psychology, Childhood Education,
Child Study, The Grade Teacher, Journal of Education,
Journal of Geography, Journal of Higher Education,
Latin Notes, Loyola Digest, The Mathematics Teacher,
Mental Hygiene, School Executives Magazine, were
mentioned once.

* The large number given for the N. E. A. Journal is probably due to
membership drives, subscription to the magazine following automatically.

Of the general magazines, the following were mentioned two or
more times:

Literary Digest   18
Atlantic Monthly   14
Time   12
World's Work   10
Forum   9
Reader's Digest   9
Harper's Magazine   8
Survey   8
New Republic   7
Current History   6
Nation   6
Review of Reviews   4
New York Times (Sunday)   4
Outlook   3
American Mercury   2
World Tomorrow   2
Scribner's   2

The American Magazine, Colliers, Historical Outlook,
The North American Review, Pathfinder, Plain Talk,
The Saturday Evening Post, World Unity, Yale Review,
were mentioned once.

The titles of the "five most significant books read in the past three
years" are:

Whither Mankind (Beard)   7
Practice of Teaching in Secondary Schools (Morrison) 7
America Comes of Age (Siegfried)   5
American Road to Culture (Counts)   5

A Preface to Morals (Lippmann)   5
All Quiet on the Western Front (Remarque)   4
The Child-Centered School (Rugg and Shumaker)   4
Humanity Uprooted (Hindus)   4
Our Times (Sullivan)   4
The Story of Philosophy (Durant)   4
The Art of Thinking (Dimnet)   3
Education, Crime, and Social Progress (Bagley)   3
The Human Mind (Burnham)   3
The Meaning of a Liberal Education (Martin)   3
Modern Educational Theories (Bode)   3
Middletown (Lynd)   3
Quest for Certainty (Dewey)   3
Rise of American Civilization (Beard)   3

Adult Education (J. K. Hart); The Adams Family (J. T. Adams); American Leviathan (Charles Beard); Behaviorism (J. B. Watson); Biological Basis of Human Behavior (H. S. Jennings); Brain Mechanic and Intelligence (K. S. Lashley); Giants in the Earth (O. E. Rolvaag); Human Nature and Conduct (John Dewey); Mansions of Philosophy (Will Durant); Organization of Supervision (F. C. Ayer and A. S. Barr); Psychologies of 1930 (A symposium); Passing of the Recitation (V. T. Thayer); Supervised Student Teaching (A. R. Mead); Sociological Philosophy of Education (R. L. Finney), were mentioned twice.

With this picture of the reading activities of the fifty-six theory teachers before us, what conclusions can be drawn?

In the first place, there does not seem to be a great deal of the kind of reading likely to provoke criticism of the *status quo* in education and society. Among the educational and general magazines, those of a more standard type are found at the top. The four general magazines receiving the highest votes are essentially conservative in outlook. The publications most likely to disturb complacency and stimulate thought on social problems, such as *Forum, The New Republic, The Nation* (with 9, 7, 6, votes respectively), are not read very extensively by theory teachers, *nor even considered most helpful "in understanding current social movements and events."*

The same tendency is revealed by the book list submitted. The request was made that the "five most *significant* books" be mentioned. Only seven of the fifty-six theory teachers mentioned such a thought-provoking book as *Whither Mankind*. A suggestion of the narrow educational interest of American educators is revealed by the fact that Morrison's *Practice of Teaching in Secondary*

Schools tied with *Whither Mankind* for first place among the "most significant" books read. One looks in vain in the reading list submitted for such writers as Bertrand Russell, Stuart Chase, Overstreet, Laski, George Soule, John H. Randall, and Ogburn. Counts and Lippmann were mentioned but five times each; Rugg, Hindus, and Sullivan, but four times each. James Truslow Adams was mentioned but once. Most significant perhaps is the fact that Dewey was barely mentioned.

SECTION II

PHILOSOPHIES OF THEORY TEACHERS

Probably the most important index for the purpose of appraising the teaching of general educational theory is the social and educational philosophy of the teachers. The nature of the course depends more upon the social and educational outlook of the instructors than upon the contents of the texts used. The matter of point of view is the more important in the general theory courses since they have as their primary purpose the developing of a broad view of life and of education.

With these considerations in mind this study has included an examination of the social attitudes and working concepts of teachers of general theory. For the purpose of obtaining data bearing on the social orientations of the teachers, Harper's *A Social Study* was employed. To discover the basic educational conception of the theory teachers the instrument referred to in Chapter III was formulated so as to afford an estimate of these underlying beliefs and views.

Harper's *A Social Study*[4] was devised for the purpose of estimating the degree of liberalism or conservatism of educators in the various strata of the profession. By conservatives Harper understands persons who "regard the existing distribution of wealth as essentially just . . . think that under present conditions most people get substantially what they deserve to get . . . are opposed to economic experimentation . . . say we should leave well enough alone . . . undertake to suppress the very discussion of proposed radical changes in our system of government or in our system of property holding. . . ." [112] Liberals and radicals on the other hand " 'hold that the distribution of wealth is unfair, individual failure . . . is due as often as not to the fact that the one who failed did not have a chance . . . deny that we have equality of

---

[4] A copy will be found in the Appendix.

opportunity in this country . . . want to effect decided changes in our national life so that we may be more democratic. . . .'"
[87:12]

This instrument consists of seventy-one propositions to which those tested are requested to answer Yes or No. The score on the test is a score of a person's liberalism; the higher the score, the greater the liberalism; the lower the score, the greater the conservatism. As a result of his investigation of more than three thousand educators, Harper came to the conclusion that consistency, stability, and independence of social thinking varied with degree of liberalism. The more liberal or radical a person is, the more likely he is, on the basis of Dr. Harper's study, to have a consistent attitude on social problems to maintain a high degree of stability, i.e., not shift, over a short period of time from liberalism to conservatism, or vice versa, and to possess independence of thinking, i.e., not yield over-readily to suggestion. Those who ranked low can therefore, as a rule, be characterized not only as persons who accept our present institutional set-up as final, but also as confused and less stable.[5] [87:III, IV]

Measured by their reactions to Harper's *A Social Study*, what can be said of the teachers of general educational theory who are included in this investigation? Individual scores of the fifty-six individuals studied ranged from 39 to 78, the median being 62. Thirteen, or 23 per cent of the fifty-six, attained a score of 68 or more; twenty-three, or 39 per cent of the total group, scored 60 or less. In a private interview Dr. Harper expressed the opinion that a score below 68 gives evidence of enough inconsistency of thinking to indicate serious lack of background and orientation for dealing with social problems. It will be noted that forty-three individuals, or 77 per cent of the total group, failed to make a score of 68 per cent; that 39 per cent scored below 60. It would seem, therefore, that the social thinking of teachers of general educational theory, as estimated through this instrument, is inadequate to the performance of their professional duties.

This point is further borne out by a comparison of the results ob-

[5] It will be noted that Dr. Bagley does not agree with the interpretation of "liberal" as made by Harper and Peterson. He writes liberal "seems to justify the identification of progress with mere change. Freedom of speech and freedom of the press are part and parcel of our *status quo*. Surely a 'deviation' toward the suppression of such freedom . . . would be neither 'liberal' nor 'progressive' in the sense in which most of us use these terms." For further elaboration of this point and for other significant criticisms of some features of the instruments as here used and interpreted, the reader is urged to read Dr. Bagley's article. [119]

tained in the present study with the results obtained by Harper in his investigation. Harper conducted his survey in 1922 in the era of Harding prosperity. The norms for the different educational strata obtained by him are given below:

D. Norms for Educators

More advanced Negro educators of the South (other norms, whites only)   39
Educators having not more than 4 years of education above eighth grade   41
Educators having 4 to 7 years of education above eighth grade   43
Educators holding a Bachelor's degree only, South   44
Educators holding a Bachelor's degree only, Middle and Far West   48
Graduate educators in general   50
Graduate educators after the completion of certain courses   68

On the surface it would appear that teachers of general educational theory rank fairly high in liberalism and the concomitant qualities of social thinking referred to above. The group subjected to the present study ranked higher than Harper's graduate educators in general and came close to Harper's group ranking highest in liberalism—"graduate educators after the completion of certain courses of study." Further consideration, however, would result in a less optimistic picture. In the first place there was every reason to hope that the group of teachers of educational theory would rank with "graduate educators after completion of certain courses" in general theory. The students in these courses included, besides elementary school teachers, instructors in teachers colleges, supervisors, administrators, and high school teachers. The group included in the present study, on the other hand, were all teaching on the college level and, moreover, were teaching a subject that presumably is liberalizing and thought provoking. Furthermore, it is most probable that a particular score on Harper's instrument in 1922 indicated relatively a greater degree of liberalism than the same score did in 1931, the second year of the economic crisis.

What are the *educational* philosophies of the teachers of general educational theory included in this study?

Mention has already been made of an "instrument" on issues in American education, the result of the joint efforts of Professor Raup, Dr. Peterson, and the present writer. This instrument consisted of seventy-nine propositions clustering around what the authors of the instrument considered to be some of the major considerations that underlie conflicts in contemporary thought and practice.

Some of these considerations, such as the static vs. the dynamic conception of the universe and of man, the assumption of the existence of a separate mind vs. the naturalistic view that mind is integrally related with the organism in the process of its adjustment to and reconstruction, of its environment, come within the broad area of philosophy. Another consideration is concerned with the comparative importance of heredity and environment in determining the capacities and conduct of the human individual. Still another consideration deals with the conflict between two social philosophies, one indicating increased socialization of the cultural and economic resources of the nation as both desirable and necessary and the other insisting that basically American economic individualism should still retain its primary place as the basis for conducting the affairs of the groups. Again, educators seem to be divided as to what constitutes an adequate methodological basis for criticising and reconstructing an educational program. It has already been pointed out that the major division along this line is that distinguishing those whose orientation is determined largely by the "analytical," quantitative, testing, controlled-experimental procedures of science and those who believe that a sound educational program can be arrived at only through consideration of the values in the whole of our experience, individual and social. According to this view science is an element, but only one element in the whole process. Thus the scientific vs. the philosophical approach constitutes a major issue in educational thought and practice.

Again, in so far as existing or proposed curricula methods, and systems of administration, have a consistently thought-out basis, they tend to rest either on the view which emphasizes that the learning process is active, creative in nature or on that which stresses that it is passive in nature. Without extended elaboration of this issue, it may be said that the latter view holds either that the learning process is psychologically an act of being shaped by educative situations or that the learning is most desirable and most economic when the learner receives with little creative, aggressive urge what those who are in charge of education can administer. The other view takes its cue from the recognition that all human behavior is in the nature of active adjustment in situations and that therefore the learning process is an active "reconstruction of experience" in the environment in which the learning individual is placed. Even passive learning is active according to this view; active on a superficial, uneconomical plane.

Finally, curriculum theories and practices tend to fall within two broad classes—first, those that take their point of departure from the traditional established curriculum, and second those that hold that the educational program is or should consist of a series of life activities.

In brief summary, the major issues in education are:

Static	Dynamic
Separate mind	Naturalistic view
Heredity	Environment
Traditional individualism	Socialization
Scientific	Philosophical
Academic	Direct life
Passive	Active

Broadly, therefore, and in logical extremes, there are two educational attitudes. One can be described as static, academic, narrowly scientific, traditional individualistic, passive, dualistic, based on belief in heredity. The other can be described as the dynamic, direct life, philosophic, devoted to socialization, environmentalist, active, naturalistic.

In the ensuing pages the data which will throw light on the position of the teachers of general theory with respect to each of the above major issues will be presented. [102 : III][6] The numbers before each statement are those used in the instrument.

Static—Dynamic

1. The purpose of education should be essentially to prepare boys and girls for the activities which make up, or which ought to make up, well-rounded adult life.

5. The most effective instruction results when the teacher aims primarily to prepare the child for successful adult life.

7. If the curricula of our teacher-training institutions are to be changed from their traditional academic basis, a survey of the school activities of teachers in the public schools should furnish us the basic materials for building the new curricula.

19. The best way to deal with such doctrines as communism is to teach positively the soundness of our own economic system.

[6] A copy of the instrument will be found in the Appendix.

System of scoring.—As observed, before each statement are three groups of parentheses. If the proposition is accepted as stated with no qualifications, a plus is placed in the first pair of parentheses; if accepted, but with reservations, in the second pair; if accepted but with many reservations, in the third pair. If the proposition is rejected, the minus sign is used in the same manner. Numerical values were assigned as follows: three points for no reservations, two for some reservations, one for many reservations. The papers were scored by placing the marks on one or the other side of the issue involved according to whether it was accepted or rejected.

23. Upon the public schools of America must rest, as their dominant task, the guardianship and transmission of the race heritage.

27. In this period of rapid change, it is highly important that education be charged with the task of preserving the long established and enduring educational aims and objectives.

28. In any community where opinion is predominantly one side of a certain question, the wise teacher will keep classroom discussion off that question.

33. In the interest of social stability, the members of the new generation must be brought into conformity with the enduring beliefs and institutions of our national civilization.

34. As science develops, it will some day be able to predict up to a very high degree of accuracy what a given individual will do in almost any particular situation.

40. Job analysis is a highly reliable technique for determining principles and objectives for the elementary-school curriculum.

43. Adult life changes so rapidly that it cannot safely be used to set the standards for the education of children.

48. With the extension of knowledge and the development of science, the element of uncertainty in life is being progressively decreased.

The votes of the theory teachers in terms of totals for each side and in percentages are:

Static	Dynamic
725	623
54%	46%

It is noted that the vote is nearly 50–50 with some tendency toward the static view. In other words, while there is much inconsistency and lack of clear conception of the issue involved, the theory teachers tend to lean toward the view that education is preparation for a future adult life, that teacher-training institutions and the elementary and secondary schools should construct their curricula by means of the job-analysis technique, that teachers should indoctrinate as to the soundness of American institutions and that children should conform to them, that the chief task of education is the preservation and transmission of the social heritage, that controversial questions should be kept out of the classroom. There is a failure to recognize that out of controversy and conflict, progress is born. Many of our best thinkers see in the schools one of the greatest agencies for social regeneration. To accomplish this, attention should be fixed not primarily on the buildings or the physical equipment, but on the teacher, who is, to a large extent, the product of the institution of his preparation. In the teacher-training institution, the courses upon which falls the chief burden of liberalizing and expanding the intellectual powers of the students are the general theory courses. If then, the instructors of these courses are at sea on such an issue as the one under present consideration, and even indicate a preference for the static conception, with what confidence can the American people look to their schools as the hope of the future?

Separate Mind—Naturalistic View

35. In putting so much emphasis upon the psychology of habit and learning, we are failing to cultivate the human will which gives expression to the real self of the individual.

37. It is the influence and pressure of the social group which brings the individual to feel personally responsible, and there is no other source of such feeling of responsibility.

56. To think of motive as a part of the act performed is truer than to think of motive as back of and impelling the act performed.

59. The individual is born with a mind which serves him throughout life as an agent for acquiring and retaining knowledge.

61. To believe the spirit of man, like his body, is simply a part of nature is to deny him the possibility of enjoying the finer things in life.

62. Mind is individual; that is, each person has his own mind which is not only distinct from the minds of all other persons, but is also set apart from the world to be known.

65. In man's experience there are two realms: one an inner, characterized by mind; the other an outer, characterized by mere physical activity.

68. I consider that man has a two-fold nature, consisting of body and soul.

71. To say that an individual has a soul is only to call attention to certain characteristics of his ways of feeling and acting as a human organism.

74. It is more true to say that the self *is* the habits acquired by the individual in the course of his life than to say that the self must be there to acquire the habits.

76. Man's faculty of reason is complete in itself apart from the subject matter upon which man applies his reason.

77. Moral principles come from a source outside ourselves, and as such should be the determiners of changing social conditions rather than determined by them.

The vote on this category is:

Separate Mind	Naturalistic View
561	951
37%	63%

While a heavier vote was cast for the naturalistic view, there is sufficient lack of consistency to justify the conclusion that on this issue, also, the theory teachers have not thoroughly sensed the implications of their beliefs. There is considerable ambiguity as to the nature of the self, as to whether the mind is a separate entity. A considerable percentage of teachers still hold to the dualistic, body-soul conception of the individual.

Heredity—Environment

54. It is misleading to believe that anyone is a "born teacher."
57. Education may well be conceived as the unfolding of what is latent in the child.
60. Environmental influences, more than heredity, determine the differences in mental ability which children show.
63. The people of some nations possess on the average a greater native capacity for learning languages than do the people of some other nations.
66. Man's inborn tendency to fight makes it highly improbable that war can ever be entirely abolished.
69. As far as capacity for education is concerned, one race is practically as capable of higher civilization as another.
72. Classes in society are determined largely by conditions which are biologically inherent, hence social stratification must be accepted in any social order.
75. The source of economic competition is found in the trait of acquisitiveness in man's original nature.
78. Orphan infants adopted into very desirable homes sometimes turn out disappointingly. I consider that in most such cases original nature is probably a more potent factor than environment.
79. The dominance of the white race in the world today bespeaks a mental capacity superior to that of other races.

In this category the theory teachers score:

Heredity	Environment
491	613
44%	56%

In the main these instructors do not definitely declare themselves as to whether education is the unfolding of latency, whether war is instinctive and therefore irrevocable, whether classes in society are relatively fixed due to biological heredity, whether economic competition and capitalism are instinctive and thus must always remain central in human culture, whether certain races are biologically superior to others. On these questions, fraught with such significant consequences for the future development of society, it would seem that teachers of general educational theory should arrive at a more definite position. There is evidence here of an outgrown psychology and a failure to become informed on the newer developments of biology and sociology.

Traditional Individualism—Socialization

4. In educating the youth of our country we have indeed put emphasis upon individual success, but we have done so with due consideration for social good.
8. Each state should be free to order its own education without being obliged to heed the decisions of any system of national planning commissions.
14. It is sound practice to apportion state school funds to local communities according to the amounts those communities are already spending for their schools.
22. The school should strive to develop in its pupils that hardy and rugged individualism which characterized early American life.
26. With increasing interdependence within our national life, there is need for some type of central agency to effect a corresponding increase in unification of educational effort.
32. By means of a system of nation-wide planning commissions, the United States should undertake deliberately to shape and give direction to the course of its social development.
39. The first concern of the teaching profession in America should be with the understanding and control of the forces that are making a new society.
42. The effectiveness of education should be determined more by general social conditions (such, for instance, as revealed through crime statistics) than by any apparent effect upon particular individuals.
46. Without passing upon the merits of communism, we might find a valuable suggestion for us in Russia's current use of her public schools in carrying out a deliberately planned social program in the nation.
51. Any organization of education of higher official standing than that now represented by the Office of Education in Washington, D. C., would tend unduly to jeopardize the rightful control by states and local communities over their own education.

The theory teachers again favor the right side:

Traditional Individualism	Socialization
381	771
33%	67%

About one third of the votes indicate the belief that state school funds should be apportioned according to the effort expended rather than the need, that bureaucracy is feared in national control of schools, that the schools should not be used for a deliberately planned social program, that the school should continue to prepare for an individualistic, rather than a coöperative society.

Science—Philosophy

9. The place given to specific techniques and measurements in the professional education of teachers today should be reduced rather than increased.
18. For some types of problems in education, the philosophic and not the scientific method must remain permanently the guide to a solution.
21. We must come to rely chiefly upon scientific method to give us adequate educational objectives.
25. The time will probably come when the major objectives of education will be determined by persons recognized as experts in the science of education.
30. The increasing use of scientific method in the study of education will ultimately lead to the abandonment of philosophy of education.
31. A course in general educational theory can be as close to the vital and immediate needs of the prospective teacher as is the provision for his technical training and supervised practice.
36. The need for courses in general educational theory in teacher-training institutions should gradually disappear as a growing science of education shall continually improve our techniques and objective tests and measures.
44. Seeing that "natural philosophy" has been superseded by the exact sciences, we may expect that philosophy of education will eventually be superseded by the science of education.
45. General theory frequently fails to become operative in the teachers' practice because it is by nature so abstract as to prove functionally effective for only a few of the gifted students.
49. For the prospective teacher to have a good course in general principles of education and no specific training would be better than for him to have only the technical specific training and no course in general principles of education. (Supposing he could have only one or the other.)
53. The success of exact science in achieving control and mastery of mechanical things is an indication of what may be expected when the methods of the exact sciences are applied to the fields of human and social phenomena.

The total vote of the theory group is:

Science	Philosophy
508	875
37%	63%

The score substantially favors the "right" side. This is partly due to the fact that the six propositions concerning the place of theory courses in the teacher-training curriculum are included in this category; it is to be expected that this group would favor their own courses. Therefore, it is the more surprising to find one third of the group preferring courses in techniques and measurements to courses in general educational theory, and the scientific method to the philosophic.

To the writer, it is a serious matter that so large a number of theory teachers are apparently unaware of the function and importance of philosophy in the study of education. It exhibits a serious lack of confidence in the possibility of philosophy making any significant contribution to society, and reveals a failure to perceive the corresponding possibilities of their own courses.

Academic—Direct Life

2. For the elementary school, I favor a curriculum which in large part represents an organization in terms of separate subjects.
3. Systems of uniform examinations given by boards of education in some states should be eliminated from the American public school.
6. The movement to substitute "activities" for "subjects" in the school curriculum will operate against the best interests of American education.
10. The remedy for the overcrowded curriculum in the elementary school is a program of carefully selected minimum essentials in the various subjects calling for greater mastery of fewer details.
12. Courses in the classics and in mathematics still remain among the most effective agencies of mental development in the student.
16. Education should work toward the goal of teaching and learning things when the need for them arises in life experiences.
17. College entrance requirements are too academic in character for the good of our secondary schools.
24. Telling children about the good behavior that is expected of them and urging them to follow such precepts is a procedure justified by the results which it produces in conduct.
29. The pupil profits largely in the degree that there is logical organization of the materials of instruction presented to him.
38. It is impossible to predict the adult needs of the contemporary school

population with sufficient accuracy to justify an educational program based on minimum essentials of subject matter.

41. The finer phases of culture are best pursued for their own sake, and should, on the whole, be kept separate from matters of practical and vocational development.

52. The scholastic attainments of pupils as revealed by standardized achievement tests constitute a reliable basis upon which to rate the teachers of those pupils.

The votes of the theory teachers on this category are:

Academic	Direct Life
422	1,036
29%	71%

Here a strong leaning is shown toward the direct-life idea, a somewhat pronounced reversal of the position registered on the category, static–dynamic; for "academic" education is essentially static in import as the similarity between the propositions of the categories reveals. The entire group of 551 instructors tended to vote heavier on the "right" side of this category than on any other. As explained by Peterson, this is probably due to the fact that these propositions were couched in the language of the classroom and frequently in the slogans and catch phrases current in the present educational literature. The theory teachers have revealed themselves as favoring "activities" rather than "subjects," education conceived in terms of present rather than future needs. They are opposed to large-scale uniform examinations, to "minimum" essentials, to the classics and mathematics as means of mental development, to college entrance requirements, to exhortation as the means of securing good moral character, to logical organization of subject matter.

Passive—Active

11. We should cease to put emphasis upon education in childhood for the deferred values of later life.

13. The school should instill obedience, for it is a condition of the highest type of leadership that "he who would command must first learn to obey."

15. The years of childhood should be thought of as being primarily a period of preparation for adult life.

20. Some children who are fully normal mentally are quite incapable of creative endeavor.

47. Little of value can be achieved in the education of children until they have learned obedience to those in authority.

50. As a rule, drill should be introduced only in situations where the pupils feel a genuine need for it.

55. I believe that it is *often* desirable to subordinate the good in the child's present living to the greater good of his future adult life.

58. The school will fail to measure up to its responsibilities in reducing crime in the degree that it gives up its well established principles of discipline to make way for greater pupil freedom.

64. In teaching such subjects as geography and history, I favor the following procedure: protest, teach, test the result, adapt the procedure, teach and test again to the point of actual learning.

67. Educational experts rather than classroom teachers should make the curriculum.

70. Children from the first school years on should be given a genuine determining part in selecting the activities of their school curriculum.

73. Coercion is necessary in schools because a good curriculum must call for the learning of many things whose value the young pupil cannot yet appreciate.

The score for this category is:

Passive	*Active*
631	786
45%	55%

As noted in the statements, the ideas involved here bear considerable resemblance to those in the static–dynamic and academic–direct life categories. In the issue static–dynamic, the theory group voted heavier on the "left" side; in academic–direct life, a heavy majority for the "right"; and in this category the vote was more nearly 50-50.

Many of these issues have not been thought through. There should be greater consistency among them.

In this category opinion is divided as to whether education should center its attention upon present life or the "deferred values of later life," whether children should be taught to obey (which means essentially conformity to adult ways, and negates thinking and creativity), whether some normal children are "incapable of creative endeavor," whether "discipline" or "freedom" should prevail in the classroom, whether pupils and teachers should collaborate in the construction of the curriculum.

Table IX presents a summary of the votes by categories of the teachers of general educational theory, the votes of the entire group, and of the "Professors."[7]

[7] For purposes of comparison, the instrument was marked by thirty professors of Teachers College, Columbia University. An effort was made to secure a fair representation of the school.

TABLE IX

COMPARISON ON EACH OF THE SEVEN CATEGORIES BY TOTAL VOTES
AND PERCENTAGES OF THE ENTIRE GROUP OF INSTRUCTORS
(551), THE TEACHERS OF GENERAL EDUCATIONAL
THEORY (56), AND "PROFESSORS"

	Entire Group of Instructors		Teachers of General Education Theory		"Professors"	
Static–Dynamic	8,787–5,947		725–623		189–404	
	60%	40%	54%	45%	42%	68%
Academic–Direct Life	5,563–9,224		422–1,036		105–673	
	38%	62%	29%	71%	16%	84%
Science–Philosophy	5,827–7,417		508–875		129–532	
	44%	56%	37%	63%	20%	80%
Traditional Individualism– Socialization	4,693–6,927		381–771		114–414	
	40%	60%	33%	67%	22%	78%
Heredity–Environment	7,053–5,215		491–613		223–334	
	57%	43%	44%	56%	40%	60%
Passive–Active	7,418–6,837		631–786		171–461	
	53%	47%	45%	55%	27%	73%
Separate Mind–Naturalistic View	7,574–7,417		561–951		120–543	
	50%	50%	37%	63%	18%	82%
Total	46,915–48,984		3,719–5,655		1,051–3,361	
	49%	51%	40%	60%	24%	76%

It is observed that the theory group voted· heavier on the "right" side, and as such more closely approximates that of the "professors." In so far as it can be assumed that the "professors" represent a more carefully thought-out position, and in so far as the "right" side represents a more liberal point of view (as demonstrated by Peterson's study of correlation with the Harper instrument), this is encouraging. But as expressed by Peterson in reference to the votes of the theory teachers, "this probably leaves much to be desired." The highest "right" side vote was cast in the Academic–Direct Life category and the lowest "right" side vote for Static–Dynamic.

In the total scores for all seven categories the entire group of instructors approximates a 50–50 vote; the theory group, showing more definiteness of viewpoint, register 40 to 60; while the "professors," revealing still greater consistency of position, vote 24 to 76.

One of the most significant conclusions to be drawn from this comparison of scores is the failure on the part of theory teachers to differentiate clearly the various philosophic positions in current education. There seems to be a most indiscriminate "picking and choosing," a failure to sense the contradictions involved.

The result of fourteen interviews with teachers of general educational theory confirms the above conclusions. One individual expressed his views in this manner: "I don't believe in basing my theories on any one man or any one 'school'. I like to use my own judgment and choose the ideas I like the best. It makes no difference to me whether Bagley, Morrison, or Kilpatrick says it. If I like it, I take it." His score on the instrument showed him to be a true "straddler" with approximately a 50–50 vote.

The conclusions drawn by Peterson [102:122] as a result of the total scores are in the main true also of the theory group:

"1. To a significant degree, teachers are not aware of the more subtle implications and assumptions which underlie the positions for which they declare themselves on the various issues.

"3. Teacher opinion is in considerable degree "sloganized" in the case of educational trends and it is evident that, in many instances, teachers have little more than a verbal acquaintance with the movements which have been extensively advocated.

"4. Many teachers lack a unified point of view. That is, they have not formulated a well-ordered, thought-out philosophic outlook in terms of which to judge problems and issues."

These are criticisms of the thinking of the entire group of instructors included in this investigation but they are the more serious in the case of the instructors of general educational theory.

CHAPTER V

SUGGESTIONS CONCERNING FUNCTION, CONTENT, AND TEACHING OF GENERAL EDUCATIONAL THEORY

SECTION I

THE FUNCTION OF PHILOSOPHY OR GENERAL THEORY OF EDUCATION

PROMINENT among the points made in objection to courses in general educational theory was that such courses are not of "practical" value in the actual teaching process. Whether such a contention is or is not valid depends upon the meaning of "practical." If by "practical" is meant something that can be immediately utilized in teaching conventional subject matter, in the management of school routine, in the preparation of school budgets, general educational theory is not practical. If, on the other hand, our notion of "practical" is broad enough to include those activities which, while they do not promise to be immediately effective, yet contain the possibility of enhancing the contributions of the teacher to individual and social life, general educational theory *is* practical.[1]

If it is practical to know what one is about, courses in general theory, inasmuch as it is their chief function to clarify educational purposes, should rank among the most practical in the teacher-training curriculum. More than ever is such a process of clarification called for today. There is no longer an agreement as to what school education should do. Instead the educator is confronted with various conflicting purposes that have prevailed in the past. He faces

---

[1] "The most specific thing that educators can do first is something general. The first need is to become aware of the kind of world in which we live; to survey its forces; to see the opposition in forces that are contending for mastery; to make up one's mind which of these forces come from a past that the world in its potential powers has outlived and which are indicative of a better and happier future. The teacher who has made up his mind on these points will have little difficulty in discovering for himself what specific things are needed in order to put into execution the decisions that he has arrived at. Justice Holmes once said that theory was the most practical thing in the world. This statement is pre-eminently true of social theory of which educational theory is a part." [130]

the many conflicting demands of the present social order. What is
he to do? How shall he determine the direction of his work?

To answer these questions he must get beyond the schoolroom.
He must scrutinize life and the demands life makes upon the individual. He must scrutinize society to see what demands society
makes upon education. Such considerations raise the question:
What in life is most worth striving for? They raise questions as
to the nature of the good society. How can individuals living together in a given area manage themselves as a group in such a way
that all may more nearly achieve the highest satisfactions life has to
offer? Unless teachers give conscious thought to the matter of
purposes, unless they make an honest and deliberate effort to develop a point of view about life and society, their practice will be
stupid, opportunistic or aimless, or bound by ideals long since rendered obsolete by the course of changing events.

In the sense, then, of helping the teacher formulate more adequate purposes to guide his work, the study of the theory of education should be a most practical activity. Dewey thus urges the practical value of theory:

"Theory is in the end, as has been well said, the most practical of
all things, because this widening of the range of attention beyond
near-by purpose and desire eventually results in the creation of wider
and farther-reaching purposes and enables us to use a much wider
and deeper range of conditions and means than were expressed in
the observation of primitive practical purposes. For the time being,
however, the formation of theories demands a resolute turning aside
from the needs of practical operations previously performed." [81:
17]

Closely related to the matter of the practicality of general educational theory is the problem of the working relations of theory and
practice. The present investigation revealed that many object to
courses in general theory because they are "too far removed from
practice." Students are often heard to say they do not want "theory"—they want "something practical." On the street one often
hears: "That may be a beautiful theory, but it won't work in practice." Or "What we need to run the government is not a lot of
theorists, but practical business men." On every hand this dualistic
conception of the separation of theory and practice is to be found.

This separation of theory and practice is related to other dual-
isms, such as body and mind, thought and action. An intensive discussion of this problem cannot be attempted in the present work.

In order to show that there is no separation of theory and practice in life, but that they are two phases of the same process, let a simple illustration be cited in the teaching of history:

Teacher A teaches American history for no other reason than that he believes everyone should "know the facts of American history." This, in reality, is a particular theory. It is the theory, namely, that his function as a teacher is to impart the facts of history; it is the theory that knowledge *per se* is the greatest good and the aim of education. The teacher may not be conscious that this theory underlies his practice; he may even ridicule theory and insist that in his practice theory has no place, but his procedures in the teaching of history are part and parcel of this theory of education. The methods he uses in assigning lessons, in conducting recitation, in giving examinations and tests, all are determined by his theory. Lessons will be assigned, for example, requiring the memorization of a number of facts and the recitation will be conducted chiefly to test the pupil's success or failure in acquiring the assigned information. According to this theory, success in teaching is measured in terms of the number of facts reported in class recitations or on examinations.

Teacher B may believe American history should be taught to develop patriotism. History should develop pride of country and loyalty to its institutions. This theory will govern his selection of textbooks, the type of material emphasized in class, the interpretation that will be given to various events in American history. For example, he would prefer, no doubt, textbooks which magnify American heroes, demonstrate the virtues of the United States government, and endorse without exception its domestic and foreign dealings. Class discussions will likewise tend to glorify all things American. There would be little disposition to criticize any act of the government in the past or even to reveal all the facts involved in the various situations. Those facts which do not redound to the credit of American statesmen and American policies would be slighted or overlooked entirely.[2]

Teacher C may believe the function of American history is not to present facts to be learned, not to develop 100% Americans. He may operate on the theory that the function of history is to develop *intelligent* citizens whose understandings and attitudes are adequate for life needs today. He lays stress on those problems of United

[2] The usual teaching of conditions leading to the Mexican and Spanish-American wars are cases in point.

States history most likely to be of value in solving present problems. Because the attitudes he wishes to develop are different from those of Teacher B, different texts will be selected, different subject matter will be emphasized, different methods of recitation will be employed and different interpretation will be made of the facts studied. Teacher C may also have a theory that the study of history should produce more effective thinking. To this end he might use every opportunity to develop critical mindedness by helping his pupils to criticize both favorably and adversely the various acts of the government. He might allow the discussion of various controversial aspects of American history. He might try to teach his pupils to form judgments only after all available evidence has been considered and after recognizing the dangers of harmful prejudice. Because, then, of his educational theories, Teacher C, it is seen, is concerned with teaching certain knowledges of American history, with developing certain attitudes toward the United States and toward United States history, and with developing certain habits of thinking.

In each of these cases it is seen that theory and practice are integrally related. The practice is rooted in the theory and the two cannot be separated. One teacher requires that his pupils memorize the facts of the Spanish-American War. The other directs attention to factors in society that caused the War and to factors present in civilization that perpetually tend to produce all wars. In each case there are different theories and different practices. It is not a case of whether or not theory or practice is to be preferred, but rather *which theory* is to be preferred.

But if theory and practice are thus interwoven in the activities of the teacher, how can one justify a separate course in general educational theory? Let us suppose that Teacher A comes in contact with Teacher C. Teacher C says that he teaches history not for the sake of history, but for its usefulness in the lives of the people. He may insist his first concern is with the individual, his interests, his needs, how he learns. History, he may urge, should develop certain appreciations of the good, the true, and the beautiful in American history; it should open the eyes of the pupils to certain factors at work in the conduct of group life that militate against the welfare of the underprivileged classes. It should develop attitudes of critical-mindedness and open-mindedness. It should reveal the function of coöperation in achieving the common good.

Such considerations as these may cause Teacher A to reflect on his own theoretical position, to question the adequacy of the theory that knowledge of history is its own justification and to seek for other values to be achieved in the teaching of history. This process of reflecting upon the broader aspects of his work requires a certain detachment from the actual immediate process of teaching history, but always with the end in view of making his teaching more significant. It requires him to consider the individual and his needs, society and its needs, and other basic questions, not, however, isolating his thought from the problems of the history teacher. When he does this he is doing what this thesis holds courses in general educational theory should do; that is, deliberate upon all pertinent considerations involved in the educative process. To help the student get outside the narrow confines of the merely immediate things of education and to consider their broader bearings in individual and group life is the function of the course in general educational theory. It draws the attention temporarily away from the concrete problems of teaching in order to bring to these problems the broader considerations which must be included if the concrete situation is to be handled most intelligently. To theorize, then, about the teaching of history (or any other subject) is a practical thing. In the sense that the process finds its origin in practice, tries to view the consequences of practice, and returns to practice and gives it direction, theory is seen as a phase of the total activity.

A course in general theory is properly not one isolated from practice, but rather one deeply, integrally involved with practice and detached for the purpose primarily of seeing relations among events and values, and of gathering into the service of life's course the products of our own and others' experiences. The separate course is a device for furthering and expanding this natural function of reflection. When it loses the character of practicality, it is in a pathological condition. This bad condition, and not the course with its function, should be eliminated.

SECTION II

SUGGESTIONS ON THE CONTENT OF A COURSE IN THE GENERAL THEORY OF EDUCATION

If, then, it is held that the general theory of education merits consideration in a separate course, what are some of the problems with which it should deal? No attempt will be made here to present a complete outline of such a course but merely to indicate some of the major considerations with which it should concern itself. No course in general educational theory fulfils the function indicated in the previous section unless it dwells on:

1. *The need for a point of view in education.* This topic should indicate how viewpoints develop and how they function in education. It should include the considerations to be taken into account in forming a point of view.

2. *Present economic and social conditions and ideals of American democracy.* This topic should help the student become aware of the economic maladjustments and other factors at work in modern industrial society which are rapidly transforming the conditions of life.

3. *Suggested method of social and economic reconstruction.* After the student is made sensitive to the conditions which prevail, he is ready to consider some of the various proposals that have been offered and the dangers (if any) as well as the advantages that lie in these proposals.

4. *Rôle of the school in social reconstruction.* This topic should introduce the student to the failure of the school in the past to play any vital part in directing social change and to the responsibilities imposed upon the school by present conditions.

5. *Nature of the individual and his relation to society.* This topic should include a discussion of the dualistic vs. the naturalistic view of human nature, the experimental nature of intelligence, the rôle of interest in learning, logical vs. psychological subject matter, the development of appreciations and creativity, and moral education.

6. *How the considerations of the above will affect school procedures, curriculum, administration, etc.* This topic should bring the student nearer the classroom situation and should include discussion of such concrete aspects of teaching as the giving of marks and grades, the place of set courses of study, the management of classroom activities, the furnishings of the school.

The course in general should develop a vital interest in the problems of contemporary society, in the various conflicts to be found in almost every phase of it, and in the dynamic rôle of institutionalized education in the solution of these conflicts.

SECTION III

SOME SUGGESTIONS FOR IMPROVING THE EFFECTIVENESS OF THE GENERAL THEORY COURSE

1. To bridge the gap which so often exists between theory and practice, it is important that the instructor, in addition to having

made a thorough study of the history and philosophy of education, shall have had considerable public school experience. The constant employment of such experience in illustrating the various theories under discussion will give meaning to the theories. It may be that the concreteness of educational science courses is responsible for their greater effectiveness as compared with educational theory courses. If the instructor is alert to every opportunity to utilize pertinent items from his experience both as pupil and as teacher in the public school, it is likely that general theory will be more functional.

2. A theory course should be stimulating rather than didactic. It is essential that the theory course offer many challenges to the student's own thinking. By causing the student to reflect upon his experience as an elementary or secondary school pupil, or as a cadet teacher, the general theory course can contribute considerably in developing teachers who are *thinking* persons. Also, the more the new ideas presented by the theory course are connected with the familiar experiences of the students the less danger of isolation from practice.

3. The student should be introduced in the course of his study of general theory to reading material that deals with both the abstract and the concrete aspects of education. In contrast with the more abstract discussion of Dewey, there are available such concrete presentations as are to be found in Collings, *An Experiment with a Project Curriculum,* Rugg and Shumaker, *The Child Centered School,* Porter, *The Teacher in the New School,* Lane, *A Teacher's Guide to the Activity Program,* and Lincoln Elementary School, *Curriculum Making in an Elementary School.*

4. What is, perhaps, the most important of all is the realization that a working agreement of educational philosophy between the education department and the training school is necessary to the full functioning of both. To that end a close relationship between them is at all times essential. Without this it is doubtful if the theory course can function to any great extent. It will readily be seen that if the instructor of educational theory is seeking to develop one point of view and the training school is practicing another, the theory instruction can hardly be anything but futile. On the other hand, if there is considerable agreement between the two, both having essentially the same philosophy of education, the practice school serves to illustrate the theories discussed in the philosophy course and shows the student how to apply them. Student observation,

student teaching under expert supervision, and individual and group conferences with critic teachers, when conducted with the end in view not only of fixing technique but also of giving concrete meaning to. educational theory, give added significance to the training school. On the other hand, if the instructor of general theory maintains close contact with the activities of the training school, he will have at hand a rich fund of concrete material upon which to draw for illustrations and applications of theory. It is difficult to overestimate the importance of a close working relationship of the teacher of theory, or the entire education department for that matter, with the campus training school.

5. Unless the general theory course is tested as to how it functions in the elementary and secondary school, such a course can fall far short in its task of making teachers more intelligent. By means of correspondence, visits to the young teacher while at work, individual or group conferences held in connection with state or district educational meetings, the teacher of general theory can investigate the degree in which his former students are able to practice the theories about their class work discussed in his classes, and discover the difficulties which seem to stand in the way of a more general application of these theories. Such contacts should furnish many valuable illustrations of theory and many suggestions for rendering the theory course more effective.

CHAPTER VI

SUMMARY OF FINDINGS AND RECOMMENDATIONS

SECTION I

SUMMARY OF FINDINGS

ON THE basis of the material presented in the above chapters, a number of conclusions drawn from the history of general educational theory courses and their present status may be made.

1. *The actual philosophy of American education* has been shaped by the experience of the American people and by ideas imported from Europe. At any period the dominant ideas and ideals of the people have been reflected in the aims and procedures of the school. When the dominant ideal was the religious ideal of preparation for the life to come, the main function of the school was to equip the individual with the means of salvation. The theories underlying school discipline and the curriculum itself were largely derived from this conception of the destiny of man. But other factors tended to expand this ideal. The presence of a continent that invited exploitation and conquest was a vital force in laying the foundations of American attitudes and ideals in education as well as other aspects of American life. Very early the aims of individual success were reflected in the philosophy of American education. The English tradition of democracy, reinforced by the ideas of the liberal French thinkers, added the ideal of democratic citizenship. As the utilitarian democratic motifs became stronger, the Christian goal lost prominence in education.

Of the foreign ideas to influence the theory of education, the earliest to arrive were those of Pestalozzi. During the first decades of the nineteenth century and more prominently during the '60's and '70's when the Oswego movement gave vogue to some of the mechanical aspects of his pedagogy, American educational theory was challenged and modified by Pestalozzi's educational philosophy. Succeeding Pestalozzi among the European thinkers who influenced the theory of education were such figures as Hegel and Herbart. Their philosophies, though foreign, seemed to fit with the American outlook. Pestalozzian emphasis on the individual was consistent with the spirit of American individualism. Hegel's transcendentalism had a definite appeal to persons who desired to retain the beliefs of Christianity in an age when the literal acceptance of its beliefs became increasingly difficult. The Herbartian emphasis on the social aspects of education fitted in with the growing interest in society, which became more and more pronounced as the frontier disappeared and society became more complex. Toward the turn of the twentieth century American philosophies of education began to take form. Whether it was the pragmatic, democratic, and social philosophy of Dewey or the more limited philosophy reflected in the methods and aims of science and industry, they represented the spirit and ideals of American life. Whereas Dewey made explicit the meaning of the native experience, the scientific-industrial-practical educational philosophy reflected the ideals of science and big business. There can be no doubt that both bore intrinsically the stamp of America.

The general educational theory taught during the periods of our history to the present time has been thus a mixture of the European and American influences with a growing emphasis on the latter.

2. *A further relation* can be seen between the importance attributed to general educational theory in teacher-training institutions, or the teaching of general theory at any period, and the character of the period. When there is conflict in society, when hitherto accepted ways of doing things do not bring desired results, when tradition is challenged by new ideas, there is more interest in theory and particularly the theory of education. Up to 1860 there was little conscious recognition of general theory. The prevailing religious, economic, and social beliefs were accepted without largely effective question. With the introduction, however, of Pestalozzian, Hegelian, and more particularly Herbartian philosophies, traditional educational theories were challenged; the teaching of general theory rose increasingly in importance. It maintained a relatively large position until the rise of the scientific movement in education with its emphasis on measuring and testing and its correlative tendency to abandon theory as such.

In spite of the fact that social change was rapid during the decades of the present century and the *status quo* was challenged in many ways, courses in general theory declined in importance. This was in part due to the powerful sweep of the scientific movement, which, along with the tremendous physical conquests of the period, became the dominant characteristic of American civilization. Industrial growth and the scientific method crowded out all other considerations.

It is only with the crash of economic arrangements in the past few years that there has come about an increase in the importance attached to general theory of education. Belief in the techniques of science as a means of social and educational salvation has been weakening. The belief that a decent social order can be achieved with each member of society pursuing his own unsocialized ends is rapidly breaking down. Today there is no dominant ideal or method for meeting current problems. Doubt, uncertainty, and confusion characterize society. Educational theory, which was geared to the philosophy of individualism and the exact scientific method, is now seeking new foundations. No longer can the goal of personal success dominate educational theory and practice. Clearly there is need for devising a new basis for education.

Of this increasing interest in educational theory there is much evidence. It is reflected in the contents of recent books, in the programs of professional associations, in the subject matter of educational periodicals. Recent books point out that a new society is now in the process of emergence under the impact of technology, that the disappearance of the frontier has relegated individualism to the past, that the old school based on the philosophy of individualism and aiming at conserving the social heritage is no longer adequate, and that, therefore, a new philosophy of education and a new school based on considerations of emerging collectivism are needed. Educational conferences show a marked increase in the interest in philosophy of education.

Periodical literature shows a shift in emphasis from "schoolmasters' problems" to the social realities which indicate the need for new departures in education. Such shift is noticeable in *School and Society* and in the publications of several educational organizations. Prior to the 1930's the tone of these publications implied acceptance of the *status quo*. Now a considerable portion of their space is devoted to a criticism of *status quo*, and to the search for an educational method whereby changes might be effected. Notable among the evidence of the shift of professional interest is the establishment of the *Social Frontier*, dedicated to the quest of an educational philosophy equal to the demands and opportunities of a collectivistic society based upon technology.

3. *There seems to be a pronounced lag* between the importance ascribed to the teaching of general educational theory by certain leaders in education and the curricular practices of teacher-training institutions.

In contrast with the evidences of revived interest in general theory, most of the teacher-training institutions of the country have continued to emphasize courses in science of education and techniques of education. Any pronounced recognition of the necessity of reformulating general theories of education upon which the school of today must be based, at least so far as curricular offerings are concerned, is absent. The various studies that have been made show a steady decline in the course that most purely represents general educational theory—principles or philosophy of education. Various kinds of psychology courses, courses in educational measurements, in the techniques of curriculum construction have continued to increase. The only compensating aspect of this situation is the increasing vogue of introduction to education and the ability of principles of teaching to maintain its position. But as has been shown, the main purpose of general educational theory is only incidental in these courses. They are offered essentially for other purposes, and, judging from studies that have been made of these courses and the contents of textbooks, they cannot serve as substitutes for courses in principles or philosophy of education.

Not only has theory played a diminishing rôle in teacher-training curricula, but a large percentage of the instructors of teacher-training institutions are skeptical of the value of general theory. Even teachers of general theory courses share this doubt. As shown by the six propositions of the instrument and the four questions in the questionnaire, approximately 50 per cent of the instructors not teaching the general courses and 33⅓ per cent of those who do teach these courses are of the opinion that general theory is of little value in the teacher-training program. Their chief objections were that general theory is "too abstract and too theoretical" and "too far removed from practice." Some were of the opinion that "common sense and experience" are fully adequate for the guidance of the teacher; that courses in general theory only tend to confuse the student by presenting conflicting values of education.

Numerous objections were raised, too, because of the actual teaching of these courses. "Too much repetition in general theory courses" was frequently mentioned. Others complained that they are "poorly taught," and are composed largely of "meaningless jargon."

That there is reason to object to general theory courses because of the way they are taught was borne out by the findings as to the professional equipment of the instructors of these courses. There was little evidence of specialized preparation for the teaching of general educational theory. The instruction in these courses is largely in the hands of those who specialized in fields having little bearing on the broader aspects of education, such as educational administration or psychology. Their major interest, it is reasonable to suppose, is not in educational theory. It seems clear that there is little recognition of philosophy of education or general theory of education as a field of specialized study.

Nor would it seem that there is much recognition on the part of the administrators of teacher-training institutions of the pertinence of the field of general educational theory to the rounded education of teachers. Staff members who were selected because of having "majored" in administration, supervision, or any of the subject-matter fields are assigned courses in general theory "on the side." It was found that most of the instructors of general theory courses had other duties and there was evidence in some cases that these other fields absorbed the major interest and attention. It seemed apparent that there is widespread practice of "farming out" courses in general educational theory to suit administrative convenience. So long as teachers of general theory courses have made no definite effort to equip themselves for teaching general theory, so long as administrators of teacher-training institutions are not sensitive to the needs of such specialization and distribute these courses among the members of their staffs with little regard for the fitness of these members to teach these courses, the charge can justly be made that they are as a rule poorly taught.

Not only did the teachers seem to be inadequately prepared for giving instruction in the theory courses, but they fell short in their social and educational philosophies of what might be reasonably expected. What happens in the classroom depends not only on the contents of textbooks used but also on the actual beliefs of the instructors. In fact, the very content of these courses, the selection of the material used, depends directly upon the philosophies of the instructors. In no other type of teacher-training course is it so important (1) that the instructor be sensitive to the fact that political, economic, and social institutions undergo constant change, (2) that he realize that these institutions must be changed to suit changing conditions of social life, (3) that he see clearly the rôle of the school in developing such attitudes in the children as will be likely to produce a society capable of changing its institutions as the need arises. In an effort to discover the sensitivity of the instructors to the pressing problems of modern social life, a test, Harper's *A Social Study*, was administered. It was pointed out that in view of the effects of the economic depression a liberal attitude might have been hoped for from instructors teaching material whose main function should be the developing of a broad view of life. This test revealed, however, that the median score of instructors of general theory in 1931 was below that made by a heterogeneous group of graduate students after taking certain courses in 1922.

The findings of the instrument which tested the educational philosophies revealed much to be desired in the educational thinking of the instructors of general educational theory. Although the instructors of theory courses scored higher than the non-theory teachers, the total score was such as to indicate that in this group, whose function it was to help students gain clear ideas about education, there was much haziness and confusion of thought. Their total score on the issues amounted to a 40–60 ratio. Very few individuals were clear-cut conservatives or clear-cut liberals. As the total score indicates, most of the teachers of theory made a score of approximately a 50–50 ratio which indicated much inconsistency, lack of awareness of the implications of the various positions to which they subscribed, much compartmentalized thinking, and a definite lack of a unified point of view. If the main function of courses in the general theory of education is to clarify the points of view of the students, it seems probable that so long as the instructors are themselves thus confused, the courses will fall short of this objective and fail to develop the clarity of thinking so sorely needed at this time.

SECTION II

RECOMMENDATIONS

1. All public school teachers need to give conscious attention to the development of a personal philosophy of education adequate to meet the needs of our time. It is not enough that the teacher possess mastery over the techniques of teaching and testing, or that he operate on the basis of plans and specifications handed to him from supervisors, administrators or curriculum makers. He must himself possess the proper philosophic orientation to the conflicting problems of present-day society.

2. To secure this orientation, at least one course completely devoted to general educational theory should be required in all teacher-training curricula. This does not mean merely a course in introduction to education or in principles of teaching. These courses are important in the education of teachers, but the teaching of the broadly theoretical aspects of education is not their primary function. Neither does it seem that the integration type of course is adequate. This type of course collects data from the various specialized sciences and attempts to show the relation to education. This is desirable as far as it goes. A course is needed, however, which is not restricted by the academic disciplines, but which includes these and draws upon every available resource pertinent to the developing of a point of view about life and education.

3. Under the present set-up the course in principles or philosophy comes nearest fulfilling these purposes. As shown by the catalog study, however, this course should be reorganized and reoriented to accomplish these functions. It is not known what forms teacher training may assume in the future. Changes are under way as illustrated by New College, Columbia University. Nevertheless, whatever form it may take, there is need for the type of treatment which general educational theory aims to give.

4. The point of departure for the course in general theory should be the conflict in social ideas which affect education; the end which such a course should serve is an improved teaching procedure which promises to aid in the resolution of this conflict. The general theory course needs to be sufficiently detached from the minutiae of teaching techniques to afford it scope for an exploration of what education is all about. At the same time, the concepts which the course employs or which it helps the students to formulate need to have a concrete schoolroom content. To secure a theory course that can function in the professional life of the teacher, coördination of theory teaching and training school practice and the testing of the content and method of the course in the context of practice and professional teaching are necessary.

5. All members of teacher-training faculties should be thoroughly grounded in the general theory of education if American teacher-training institutions are to produce elementary and secondary school teachers with attitudes and ideals adequate to meet present needs.

6. Instructors of general theory courses should be especially prepared in the philosophy or general theory of education. To have specialized only in administration or psychology is pitiably inadequate—a farce in fact. This is not to say that training in the technical and scientific aspects of education is not important, but in addition theory teachers should have a broad general culture, a thorough background in general philosophy, and history of education, and understanding of sociology and economics, and thorough training in the philosophy of education. It is essential that they be sensitive to contemporary problems and be familiar with some of the solutions that have been offered.

7. Administrators in teacher-training institutions should be aware that the teaching of general educational theory requires special preparation. They should not distribute these courses among the members of the staff without regard to their professional equipment.

8. The teacher of general educational theory should play an important part in shaping the policies of the institution. He, *more than any member of the staff*, should be aware of the demands present conditions impose upon the public school teacher and should be able to recommend policies and programs for teacher-training institutions most likely to equip the teacher for meeting these demands.

BIBLIOGRAPHY

TEXTBOOKS USED IN GENERAL THEORY COURSES

1. ABBOTT, JACOB. *Works—A Collection of Essays, Including the Teacher; Etc.* L. Tegg, 1837. 702p.
2. ADAMS, J. E. and TAYLOR, W. S. *Introduction to Education and the Teaching Process.* Macmillan, 1932. 668p.
3. BAGLEY, W. C. *Educational Values.* Macmillan, 1911. 267p.
4. BAGLEY, W. C. and KEITH, J. A. H. *Introduction to Teaching.* Macmillan, 1924. 400p.
5. BAIN, ALEXANDER. *Education as a Science.* Appleton, 1879. 453p.
6. BETTS, G. H. *Social Principles of Education.* Scribner, 1912. 318p.
7. BLACKHURST, J. H. *Introducing Education.* Longmans, 1932. 319p.
8. BODE, B. H. *Fundamentals of Education.* Macmillan, 1921. 245p.
9. BODE, B. H. *Modern Educational Theories.* Macmillan, 1927. 351p.
10. BOLTON, F. E. *Principles of Education.* Scribner, 1910. 290p.
11. BOONE, R. G. *Education in the United States.* Appleton, 1889. 402p.
12. BROCKETT, L. P. (Philobiblius, pseud.). *History and Progress of Education from the Earliest Times to the Present.* Barnes, 1859. 310p.
13. BROOKS, EDWARD. *Normal Methods of Teaching.* Lancaster, Pa., Normal, 1879. 504p.
14. BURTON, W. H. *Introduction to Education.* Appleton, 1934. 838p.
15. CHAPMAN, J. C. AND COUNTS, G. S. *Principles of Education.* Houghton, 1924. 645p.
16. CLAPP, F. L. AND OTHERS. *Introduction to Education.* Ginn, 1929. 569p.
17. COMPAYRÉ, GABRIEL. *History of Pedagogy.* Tr. by W. H. Payne. Heath, 1885. 698p.
18. COMPAYRÉ, GABRIEL. *Lectures on Pedagogy: Theoretical and Practical.* Tr. by W. H. Payne. Heath, 1887. 491p.
19. CUBBERLEY, E. P. *Introduction to the Study of Education and Teaching.* Houghton, 1925. 476p.
20. CUBBERLEY, E. P. *Public Education in the United States.* Houghton, 1919. 517p.
21. DAVIDSON, THOMAS. *History of Education.* Scribner, 1900. 292p.
22. DEGARMO, CHARLES. *Essentials of Method.* Rev. ed. Heath, 1905. 136p.
23. DEGARMO, CHARLES. *Herbart and the Herbartians.* Scribner, 1895. 268p.
24. DEWEY, JOHN. *Democracy and Education.* Macmillan, 1916. 434p.
25. DEWEY, JOHN. *Interest and Effort in Education.* Houghton, 1913. 101p.

26. DEWEY, JOHN. *My Pedagogic Creed.* Flanagan, n.d. 32p.
27. DEWEY, JOHN. *School and Society.* University of Chicago, 1899. 129p.
28. DEWEY, JOHN AND DEWEY, EVELYN. *Schools of Tomorrow.* Dutton, 1915. 316p.
29. FITCH, J. G. *Lectures on Teaching.* New ed. Macmillan, 1885. 393p.
30. FRASIER, G. W. AND ARMENTROUT, W. D. *Introduction to Education.* Scott, 1924. 274p.
31. HAILMAN, W. N. *Twelve Lectures on the History of Pedagogy.* Van Antwerp, 1874. 130p.
32. HALL, S. R. *Lectures on School-Keeping.* Ed. by A. D. Wright and G. E. Gardner. Dartmouth, 1929. 192p. (An exact reproduction of the first 1829 edition.)
33. HARRIS, W. T. *Psychologic Foundations of Education.* Appleton, 1898. 400p.
34. HART, J. S. *In the School-Room.* Eldredge, 1868. 276p.
35. HOLBROOK, ALFRED. *The Normal or Methods of Teaching.* Lebanon, O., 1859. 456p.
36. HOOSE, J. H. *On the Province of Methods of Teaching.* Bardeen, 1879. 376p.
37. HORNE, H. H. *Philosophy of Education.* Macmillan, 1905. 295p.
38. HORNE, H. H. *Philosophy of Education . . . with Special References to the Educational Philosophy of John Dewey.* Rev. ed. Macmillan, 1927. 329p.
39. HUXLEY, T. H. *Science and Education.* Appleton, 1894. 451p.
40. JUDD, C. H. *Introduction to the Scientific Study of Education.* Ginn, 1918. 333p.
41. KILPATRICK, W. H. *Foundations of Method.* Macmillan, 1925. 383p.
42. KILPATRICK, W. H. *Source Book in the Philosophy of Education.* Macmillan, 1923. 365p.
43. MCMURRY, C. A. *Elements of General Method, Based on the Principles of Herbart.* Public School Pub. Co., 1893. 201p.
44. MACVANNEL, J. A. *College Course in the Principles of Education.* Macmillan, 1906.
45. MACVICAR, MALCOLM. *Principles of Education.* Ginn, 1892. 178p.
46. MANSFIELD, E. D. *American Education, Its Principles and Elements.* Barnes, 1850. 330p.
47. MONROE, PAUL. *Textbook of History of Education.* Macmillan, 1905. 772p.
48. OGDEN, JOHN. *Science of Education.* Van Antwerp, 1879. 234p.
49. PAGE, D. P. *Theory and Practice of Teaching.* 3rd ed. Barnes, 1895. 422p.
50. PARK, M. G. *A Problem Outline for Principles of Education.* Edwards, 1928. 59p.
51. PAYNE, JOSEPH. *Lectures on the Science and Art of Education.* 3rd ed. Kellogg, 1884. 256p.
52. PETERS, C. C. *Foundations of Educational Sociology.* Macmillan, 1924. 447p.

53. QUICK, R. H. *Essays of Educational Reformers.* Clarke, 1885. 345p.
54. RANDALL, S. S. *First Principles of Popular Education and Public Instruction.* Harper, 1868. 256p.
55. ROSENKRANZ, J. K. F. *Philosophy of Education.* Appleton, 1886. (A translation of *Die pedagogik als system,* 1848, appeared first in *Journal of Speculative Philosophy,* 1872-74.)
56. RUEDIGER, W. C. *Principles of Education.* Houghton, 1910. 305p.
57. SHELDON, E. A. *Manual of Elementary Instruction for the Use of Public and Normal Classes.* Scribner, 1862. 471p.
58. SMALL, A. W. *Demands of Sociology upon Pedagogy.* (Bound with Dewey, John, *My Pedagogic Creed.*) 1929. 15p.
59. SMITH, H. I. *Education, History of Education, a Plan of Culture and Instruction.* Harper, 1842. 340p.
60. SNEDDEN, DAVID. *Educational Sociology.* Century, 1922. 689p.
61. SPENCER, HERBERT. *Education, Intellectual, Moral and Physical.* Burt, 1861. 309p.
62. SPENCER, HERBERT. *What Knowledge Is of Most Worth?* 1859. 15p.
63. TATE, THOMAS. *The Philosophy of Education or Principles and Practice of Teaching.* Kellogg, 1885. 331p.
64. THORNDIKE, E. L. *Education, a First Book.* Macmillan, 1912. 292p.
65. TOMPKINS, ARNOLD. *Philosophy of School Management.* Boston, 1895. 222p.
66. WHITE, E. E. *Elements of Pedagogy.* American Bk., 1886. 336p.
67. WICKERSHAM, J. P. *School Economy.* Lippincott, 1864. 381p.
68. WILLIAMS, S. G. *History of Modern Education.* Bardeen, 1892. 481p.

GENERAL REFERENCES

69. AMERICAN HISTORICAL ASSOCIATION. *Conclusions and Recommendations.* Scribner, 1934. 168p.
70. BAGLEY, W. C. *Education, Crime, and Social Progress.* Macmillan, 1931. 150p.
71. BARNARD, HENRY. *Pestalozzi and His Educational System.* Bardeen, n.d. 751p.
72. BEARD, C. A. AND BEARD, M. R. *Rise of American Civilization.* Macmillan, 1927. 828p.
73. BORING, E. G. *History of Experimental Psychology.* Century, 1929. 699p.
74. BURR, M. Y. *A Study of Homogeneous Grouping in Terms of Individual Variations and the Teaching Problem.* Teachers College, 1931. 69p. (Contributions to Edu. #457.)
75. CHILDS, J. L. *Education and the Philosophy of Experimentalism.* Century, 1931. 407p.
76. CLASS, E. C. *Prescription and Election in Elementary-School Teacher-Training Curricula in State Teachers Colleges.* Teachers College, 1931. 92p. (Contributions to Edu. #480.)
77. COOK, H. M. *Training of Teachers College Faculties.* George Peabody College for Teachers, 1931. 143p. (Contributions to Edu. #86.)
78. COUNTS, G. S. *American Road to Culture.* John Day, 1930. 194p.

79. COUNTS, G. S. *Social Foundations of Education*. Scribner, 1934. 597p. (American Historical Assn. Commission on the Social Studies, Part IX.)
80. DEARBORN, N. H. *Oswego Movement in American Education*. Teachers College, 1925. 189p. (Contributions to Edu. #183.)
81. DEWEY, JOHN. *Sources of a Science of Education*. Liveright, 1929. 77p. (Kappa Delta Pi Lecture Ser. #1.)
82. DEYOE, G. P. *Certain Trends in Curriculum Practices and Policies in State Normal Schools and Teachers Colleges*. Teachers College, 1934. 104p. (Contributions to Edu. #606.)
83. FRAZIER, B. W. *History of Professional Education of Teachers in the United States*. ms. 1934.
84. GORDY, J. P. *Rise and Growth of the Normal School Idea in the United States*. U. S. Bureau of Edu., Circular of Inf. #8, 1891.
85. HACKER, L. M. AND KENDRICK, B. B. *United States since 1865*. Crofts, 1932. 775p.
86. HANSEN, A. O. *Liberalism and American Education in the Eighteenth Century*. Macmillan, 1926. 317p.
87. HARPER, M. H. *Social Attitudes and Beliefs of American Educators*. Teachers College, 1927. 91p. (Contributions to Edu. #294.)
88. HILL, C. M. *A Decade of Progress in Teacher-Training*. Teachers College, 1927. 219p. (Contributions to Edu. #233.)
89. HUBBELL, L. G. *Development of University Department of Education in Six States of the Middle West*. Catholic University, 1924. 125p.
90. KANDEL, I. L., ed. *Twenty-five Years of American Education*. Macmillan, 1924. 469p.
91. KELIHER, A. V. *A Critical Study of Homogeneous Grouping*. Teachers College, 1931. 165p. (Contributions to Edu. #452.)
92. KILPATRICK, W. H. *Education for a Changing Civilization*. Macmillan, 1926. 143p.
93. KILPATRICK, W. H., ed. *Educational Frontier*. University of Chicago, 1933. 325p. (Yearbook XXI of the National Society of College Teachers of Education.)
94. KNIGHT, E. W. *Education in the United States*. Ginn, 1929. 588p.
95. KRUSE, S. A. *Critical Analysis of Principles of Teaching as a Basic Course in Teacher-Training Curricula*. George Peabody College for Teachers, 1929. 168p.
96. LEARNED, W. S. AND OTHERS. *Professional Preparation of Teachers for American Public Schools, a Study Based upon an Examination of Tax-supported Schools in the State of Missouri*. Carnegie Foundation, 1920. 475p.
97. LEE, HARVEY. *Status of Educational Sociology in Normal Schools, Teachers Colleges, Colleges, and Universities*. New York University, n.d. 88p.
98. LUCKEY, G. W. A. *Professional Training of Secondary Teachers in the United States*. Macmillan, 1903. 391p.
99. NAPIER, T. H. *Trends in the Curriculum for Training Teachers*. George Peabody College for Teachers, 1926. 139p. (Contributions to Edu. #27.)

100. NEWLON, J. H. *Educational Administration as a Social Policy.* Scribner, 1934. 301p. (American Historical Assn. Commission on the Social Studies, Part VIII.)

101. PANGBURN, J. M. *Evolution of the American Teachers College.* Teachers College, 1932. 140p. (Contributions to Edu. #500.)

102. PETERSON, FRANCIS. *Philosophies of Education Current in the Preparation of Teachers in the United States.* Teachers College, 1933. 147p. (Contributions to Edu. #528.)

103. REISNER, E. H. *Evolution of the Common School.* Macmillan, 1930. 590p.

104. REISNER, E. H. *Nationalism and Education since 1789.* Macmillan, 1927. 503p.

105. RILEY, WOODBRIDGE. *American Thought from Puritanism to Pragmatism.* Holt, 1923. 105p.

106. RUGG, E. U. *Curricula in Teachers Colleges and Normal Schools.* ms. 1934.

107. RUGG, H. O. *Culture and Education in America.* Harcourt, 1931. 404p.

108. SNEDDEN, DAVID. *Towards Better Educations.* Teachers College, 1931. 427p.

109. STRAYER, G. D. *Brief Course in the Teaching Process.* Macmillan, 1911. 315p.

110. THAYER, V. T. *Passing of the Recitation.* Heath, 1928. 331p.

111. THORNDIKE, E. L. *Educational Psychology.* Teachers College, 1913-1914. 3 vols.

112. WHITE, W. A. AND MYER, W. E. *Conflicts in American Public Opinion.* A. L. A. 1925. 28p. As quoted from 87:12.

113. WICKERSHAM, J. P. *History of Education in Pennsylvania.* Lancaster, Pa., Inquirer Pub., 1885.

PERIODICALS

114. *American Association of Teachers Colleges Yearbook.* 1924-1934.

115. *National Society for the Study of Education Yearbook.* 1904-1934.

116. *National Society of College Teachers of Education Yearbook.* 1924-1934.

117. "American Psychological Association Meeting, 1931." *New York Times,* April 19, 1931.

118. "American Psychological Association Meeting, 1934." *New York Times,* September 6, 1934.

119. BAGLEY, W. C. "What Teacher-Training Faculties Believe; an Open Letter to Doctor Raup with Reply." *Edu. Adm. and Sup.,* 20: 251-355, May 1934.

120. BARNARD, HENRY. "Institutions for the Professional Training of Teachers in the United States." *Am. J. of Ed.,* 17:651-826, 1873.

121. BOLTON, F. E. "Curricula in University Departments of Education." *Sch. and Soc.,* 2:829-41, December 11, 1915.

122. BOLTON, F. E. "Overlapping of Courses in Education." *Ed. Adm. and Sup.,* 14: 610-23, December 1928.

123. BOLTON, F. E. "Relations of the Departments of Education to Other

Departments in Colleges and Universities." *J. of Pedagogy,* 19:137-76, 1907.

124. BROOKS, EDWARD. "Centennial Thought of Normal Schools." *N. E. A. Proceedings,* 1876, p. 161.
125. BRUCE, W. F. "Place of Philosophy in Teacher-Training Programs." *Ed. Adm. and Sup.,* 17:213-23, March 1931.
126. BUTLER, N. M. "Changes of a Quarter Century." Columbia University, 1929. Pamphlet.
127. CLOW, F. R. "Rise of Educational Sociology." *J. of Social Forces,* 2:332-35, March 1924.
128. *Common School J.* "Horace Mann." 3:164-66, June 1841.
129. EBY, FREDRICK. "Educational Historians Prepare to Strike Back." *Ed.* 48:92-101, October 1927.
130. DEWEY, JOHN. "The Teacher and His World." *Social Frontier,* 1:7, January 1935.
131. EVENDEN, E. S. "What Courses in Education Are Desirable in a Four-Year Curriculum in a State Teachers College? What Should Be Their Scope?" *N. E. A. Proceedings,* 1926, p. 889-903.
132. HARRIS, W. T. "Reviews." *Ed. Rev.,* 6:84.
133. HYDE, R. E. "Overlapping of Subject Matter in Courses in Education." *Ed. Meth.,* 6:306-09, 1927.
134. JUDD, C. H. In *University of Chicago, President's Report,* 1909-10, p. 68.
135. KEITH, J. S. "Place and Scope of Sociology in Normal Schools." *N. E. A. Proceedings,* 1915, p. 765-66.
136. KELLEY, T. L. "Scientific versus Philosophic Approach to the Novel Problem." *Science,* 71:295-302, March 21, 1929.
137. MACDONALD, M. E. "Contents of the Course Introduction to Teaching." *Ed. Adm. and Sup.,* 17:9-13, January 1931.
138. MANN, C. R. "Methods of Constructing Curriculums." *Am. Assn. of Teachers Col. Yearbook,* 1924, p. 31.
139. NOBLE, S. G. "Beginnings of a Science of Education." *Sch. and Soc.,* 38:535-36, December 23, 1925.
140. NOBLE, S. G. "From 'Lectures on School-Keeping' (1829) to 'Introduction to Education' (1925)." *Sch. and Soc.,* 23:793-802, June 26, 1926.
141. OGDEN, JOHN. "What Constitutes a Consistent Course of Study for Normal Schools?" *N. E. A. Proceedings,* 1874, p. 216-29.
142. OVERSTREET, H. A. "Finding Our Philosophy." *The Thinker,* 4:12, September 1931. Quoted from 42:7-8.
143. "Report of the Chicago Committee on Methods of Instruction and Courses of Study in Normal Schools." *N. E. A. Proceedings,* 1889, p. 570-87.
144. Report of the Commission of Faculty Scholarship. "Faculty Training in the Liberal Arts College." *North Cen. Assn.* Q. 3:172-79, September 1928.
145. REYNOLDS, R. G. "Intelligence Tests in Turn Are Tested." *New York Times,* March 15, 1931.
146. RUEDIGER, W. C. "Aspects of the Professional Work in State Normal Schools." *Ed.,* 27:174-79, November 1906.

147. *School and Society*, 22:1-6, 25-9, 127-32, 441-48, 600-06, 1925.
148. *School and Society*, 40:169-77, 473-80, 512-16, 542-45, 311-14, 373-77, 105-11.
149. SNEDDEN, DAVID. "Job Analyses, Needed Foundations of Teacher Training." *Ed. Adm. and Sup.*, 10:30-36, January 1924.
150. *Social Frontier*, 1:4, October 1934.
151. TAYLOR, A. R. "Report of the Committee on Organization, Courses of Study, and Methods of Instruction in the Normal Schools of the United States." *N. E. A. Proceedings*, 1886, p. 398-400.
152. TEACHERS COLLEGE. *Report of the Dean.* June 1930, p. 124.
153. THORNDIKE, E. L. "Contribution of Psychology to Education." *J. Ed. Psychol.*, 1:6, 1910.
154. UNIVERSITY OF ILLINOIS. *Catalog*, 1895-96. p. 195.
155. University of Michigan. *Calendar*, 1879-80, p. 44-5; 1899-1900, p. 81-82; 1922-23, p. 585-603.
156. U. S. Bureau of Education. "Report of the Commissioner of Education," 1888-89. 1:294-95, 297.
157. WATSON, G. B. "Intelligence Test." *New York Times*, October 12, 1930.
158. WATSON, J. B. "What Is Behaviorism?" *Harper's*, 152:726, May 1926.

APPENDIX

THE INSTRUMENTS USED IN THE STUDY

A STUDY OF COURSES IN GENERAL EDUCATIONAL THEORY IN PROFESSIONAL SCHOOLS FOR TEACHERS

CONFIDENTIAL REPORT

This section of the study is concerned with courses in general educational theory and their status in institutions doing teacher-training work.

You are not asked to sign your name. This accords with our intention of keeping the information strictly confidential.

Part I is intended for all administrators, teachers and supervisors of normal schools, teachers colleges and departments of education in universities and liberal arts colleges.

Part II is intended for those who do administrative work in these institutions, either full or part-time.

Part III is for teachers of courses in general educational theory. (*As explained in Part I, No. 7.*)

PART I
(*For all staff members*)

1. Age........ Male........ Female........ Date........................
2. Present position ....
3. What schools have you attended?

Name of Institution	Diploma or Degree	Date Received
High School	....	....
Normal School	....	....
Teachers College	....	....
College	....	....
(Undergraduate)		
University	....	....
(Graduate)		

4. Summer schools attended during past five years.

Institution	Year
....	....
....	....

5. List titles of any extension courses you may have taken during the past five years.

....
....

6. Major subject in graduate school? ....
   a. In undergraduate school? ....
7. What courses in general educational theory have you studied? (This is meant to include any course which, in your judgment, put primary stress upon educational theory. The following titles suggest the type of course meant: philosophy of education, principles of education, theory of teaching, principles of teaching, introduction to teaching, technique of teaching, history of education, integration courses; and some types of courses in educational sociology, etc.)

Course	Institution and Instructor	Texts used	Your opinion on value of courses as preparation for teaching
....	....	....	....

8. What teaching experience have you had (including administration)?

Institution	Subjects or grades	Title of position	Number of years
....	....	....	....

9. Indicate with a check your opinion of courses in general educational theory (as now taught):
   ( ) Of practically no value in the preparation of teachers.
   ( ) Of some value, but not worth the time spent.
   ( ) Of great value.
   ( ) Indispensable in a teacher-training program.

10. State one or two important reasons for your reaction in No. 9 above ....
....

11. Rank the following courses in the order of what seems to you to be their value for prospective teachers. (Use numerals 1, 2, 3, etc., for first, second, third, etc.)
   ( ) Education sociology   ( ) History of education
   ( ) Philosophy of education   ( ) Principles of education
   ( ) Introduction to teaching   ( ) Technique of teaching
   ( ) Principles of teaching   ( ) ....

12. Do you believe that general educational theory should be taught in separate courses or that it should be taught in connection with subject-matter courses?
....

13. Name two educational magazines that you find most helpful in your work as teacher ....

14. Name not more than three general magazines that help you most in understanding current social movements and events ....

15. Give the titles of what you consider the five most significant books (of any kind) you have read in the past three years ....
....
....

PART II
(For administrators, either full or part-time)

1. Is your school a 2, 3, or 4-year institution? ....

2. Which, if any, courses in general educational theory are required of all students? (See explanation in Part I, No. 7.) ....

3. Which, if any, courses in general educational theory are elective? ....

4. What requirement, if any, is there as to sequence and year offered of courses in general educational theory? ....

5. What place is given to the study of general educational theory at faculty or staff meetings? ....

6. Who selects text books used? ....

7. With whom rests the responsibility of making and revising courses in general educational theory? ....
....

PART III

(For instructors of general educational theory; that is, those who teach many of the courses mentioned in Part I, No. 7)

1. What is your present teaching program?

   Titles of courses   *Hours per week*

   ....

   ....

2. What was your teaching program last semester (term)?

   Titles of courses   *Hours per week*

   ....

   ....

3. What school duties other than teaching do you have? (Administration, super-vision, coaching, teacher placement, etc.) ....
   a. In terms of class hours per week, about how much time do these duties require? ....

4. Indicate in the space below by using the appropriate letter which method or methods of instruction you use in your courses in general educational theory: (a) Lecture; (b) Lecture-discussion; (c) Discussion; (d) Question-answer; (e) Projects and activites; (f) Problem; (g) Student reports.
   Usually............... Often............... Seldom...............

5. Give the authors of any text or texts which you use in general educational theory ....

6. Who selects the texts used? ....

7. Do you use a syllabus?........... Your own?........... A problem-outline book?........... Your own?........... Assignment sheets?...........
   Do you require term papers?...

8. What kind of tests do you give more often, objective or essay type?..........
   .... Do you use both?................ Other types?................

9. To which educational writers (give names of not more than three) do you refer your students most often? ....
   ....

10. List not more than five of the *most important* topics in the theory courses that you give in the order of, what you conceive to be, their relative importance.
    ....

11. What, if any, conditions or influences have led you at any time to make highly significant changes in your course(s) in general educational theory?
    ....

12. State from which authors to which authors you have changed in texts and major reference materials during the time you have been teaching general educational theory ....

TEACHERS' VIEWS ON SOME PROBLEMS IN GENERAL EDUCATIONAL THEORY*

Before you begin to mark the statements, be sure to read carefully the following:

These statements involve controversial issues in education on which outstanding educators disagree widely. And on both sides are educational leaders whose opinions we must respect.

Consequently, you should think of the statements as being *neither absolutely true nor absolutely false.*

Consider your mark as an expression of your own personal opinion. Perhaps there is no "correct answer," for our best authorities hold widely differing views. We wish to know what *you* think about these matters.

Your reactions will not be scored as right or wrong; they will be taken to

* Test devised by R. B. Raup, F. E. Peterson, and Obed Williamson. Copyright, 1931, by Teachers College, Columbia University. Revised 1934.

indicate whether you declare yourself *more for one side than for the other* of these educational issues.

Directions for marking:

Be sure to mark each statement in one of the following ways:

(+) ( ) ( ) If you feel you are in full agreement with the view set forth in the statement.

( ) (+) ( ) If you agree with the view, but with a few reservations.

( ) ( ) (+) If you agree, but only with many reservations.

(—) ( ) ( ) If you are altogether opposed to the view.

( ) (—) ( ) If you are opposed, but with a few reservations.

( ) ( ) (—) If you are opposed, but with many reservations.

( ) ( ) ( ) 1. The purpose of education should be essentially to prepare boys and girls for the activities which make up, or which ought to make up, well-rounded adult life.

( ) ( ) ( ) 2. For the elementary school, I favor a curriculum which in large part represents an organization in terms of separate subjects.

( ) ( ) ( ) 3. Systems of uniform examinations given by boards of education in some states should be eliminated from the American public school.

( ) ( ) ( ) 4. In educating the youth of our country we have indeed put emphasis upon individual success, but we have done so with due consideration for social good.

( ) ( ) ( ) 5. The most effective instruction results when the teacher aims primarily to prepare the child for successful adult life.

( ) ( ) ( ) 6. The movement to substitute "activities" for "subjects" in the school curriculum will operate against the best interests of American education.

( ) ( ) ( ) 7. If the curricula of our teacher-training institutions are to be changed from their traditional academic basis, a survey of the school activities of teachers in the public schools should furnish us the basic materials for building the new curricula.

( ) ( ) ( ) 8. Each state should be free to order its own education without being obliged to heed the decisions of any system of national planning commissions.

NOTE—You are reminded not to think of these statements as definitely true or false on somebody's authority. You are merely registering your personal opinion on the controversial issues involved.

( ) ( ) ( ) 9. The place given to specific techniques and measurements in the professional education of teachers today should be reduced rather than increased.

( ) ( ) ( ) 10. The remedy for the over-crowded curriculum in the elementary school is a program of carefully selected minimum essentials in the various subjects calling for greater mastery of fewer details.

( ) ( ) ( ) 11. We should cease to put emphasis upon education in childhood for the deferred values of later life.

( ) ( ) ( ) 12. Courses in the classics and in mathematics still remain among the most effective agencies of mental development in the student.

( ) ( ) ( ) 13. The school should instill obedience, for it is a condition of the highest type of leadership that "he who would command must first learn to obey."

( ) ( ) ( ) 14. It is sound practice to apportion state school funds to local communities according to the amounts those communities are already spending for their schools.

( ) ( ) ( ) 15. The years of childhood should be thought of as being primarily a period of preparation for adult life.

( ) ( ) ( ) 16. Education should work toward the goal of teaching and learning things when the need for them arises in life experiences.

( ) ( ) ( ) 17. College entrance requirements are too academic in character for the good of our secondary schools.

( ) ( ) ( ) 18. For some types of problems in education, the philosophic and not the scientific method must remain permanently the guide to a solution.

( ) ( ) ( ) 19. The best way to deal with such doctrines as communism is to teach positively the soundness of our own economic system.

( ) ( ) ( ) 20. Some children who are fully normal mentally are quite incapable of creative endeavor.

NOTE—Again we wish to remind you not to think of these statements as definitely true or false. Even our best authorities disagree on many of the issues involved.

( ) ( ) ( ) 21. We must come to rely chiefly upon scientific method to give us adequate educational objectives.

( ) ( ) ( ) 22. The school should strive to develop in its pupils that hardy and rugged individualism which characterized early American life.

( ) ( ) ( ) 23. Upon the public schools of America must rest, as their dominant task, the guardianship and transmission of the race heritage.

( ) ( ) ( ) 24. Telling children about the good behavior that is expected of them and urging them to follow such precepts is a procedure justified by the results which it produces in conduct.

( ) ( ) ( ) 25. The time will probably come when the major objectives of education will be determined by persons recognized as experts in the science of education.

( ) ( ) ( ) 26. With increasing interdependence within our national life, there is need for some type of central agency to effect a corresponding increase in unification of educational effort.

( ) ( ) ( ) 27. In this period of rapid change, it is highly important that education be charged with the task of preserving the long established and enduring educational aims and objectives.

( ) ( ) ( ) 28. In any community where opinion is predominantly on one side of a certain question, the wise teacher will keep classroom discussion off that question.

( ) ( ) ( ) 29. The pupil profits largely in the degree that there is logical organization of the materials of instruction presented to him.

( ) ( ) ( ) 30. The increasing use of scientific method in the study of education will ultimately lead to the abandonment of philosophy of education.

( ) ( ) ( ) 31. A course in general educational theory can be as close to the vital and immediate needs of the prospective teacher as is the provision for his technical training and supervised practice.

( ) ( ) ( ) 32. By means of a system of nation-wide planning commissions, the United States should undertake deliberately to shape and give direction to the course of its social development.

( ) ( ) ( ) 33. In the interest of social stability, the members of the new generation must be brought into conformity with the enduring beliefs and institutions of our national civilization.

( ) ( ) ( ) 34. As science develops, it will some day be able to predict up to a very high degree of accuracy what a given individual will do in almost any particular situation.

( ) ( ) ( ) 35. In putting so much emphasis upon the psychology of habit and learning, we are failing to cultivate the human will which gives expression to the real self of the individual.

( ) ( ) ( ) 36. The need for courses in general educational theory in teacher-training institutions should gradually disappear as a growing science of education shall continually improve our techniques and objective tests and measures.

( ) ( ) ( ) 37. It is the influence and pressure of the social group which brings the individual to feel personally responsible, and there is no other source of such feeling of responsibility.

( ) ( ) ( ) 38. It is impossible to predict the adult needs of the contemporary school population with sufficient accuracy to justify an educational program based on minimum essentials of subject matter.

( ) ( ) ( ) 39. The first concern of the teaching profession in America should be with the understanding and control of the forces that are making a new society.

( ) ( ) ( ) 40. Job analysis is a highly reliable technique for determining principles and objectives for the elementary-school curriculum.

( ) ( ) ( ) 41. The finer phases of culture are best pursued for their own sake, and should, on the whole, be kept separate from matters of practical and vocational development.

( ) ( ) ( ) 42. The effectiveness of education should be determined more by general social conditions (such, for instance, as revealed through crime statistics) than by any apparent effect upon particular individuals.

NOTE—Please bear in mind that your reactions will not be scored as right or wrong, but will be interpreted as placing you on one or the other side of the educational issues involved.

( ) ( ) ( ) 43. Adult life changes so rapidly that it cannot safely be used to set the standards for the education of children.

( ) ( ) ( ) 44. Seeing that "natural philosophy" has been superseded by the exact sciences, we may expect that philosophy of education will eventually be superseded by the science of education.

( ) ( ) ( ) 45. General theory frequently fails to become operative in the teachers' practice because it is by nature so abstract as to prove functionally effective for only a few of the gifted students.

( ) ( ) ( ) 46. Without passing upon the merits of communism, we might find a valuable suggestion for us in Russia's current use of her public schools in carrying out a deliberately planned social program in the nation.

( ) ( ) ( ) 47. Little of value can be achieved in the education of children until they have learned obedience to those in authority.

( ) ( ) ( ) 48. With the extension of knowledge and the development of science, the element of uncertainty in life is being progressively decreased.

( ) ( ) ( ) 49. For the prospective teacher to have a good course in general principles of education and no specific training, would be better than for him to have only the technical specific training and no course in general principles of education. (Supposing he could have only one or the other, not both.)

( ) ( ) ( ) 50. As a rule, drill should be introduced only in situations where the pupils feel a genuine need for it.

( ) ( ) ( ) 51. Any organization of education of higher official standing than that now represented by the Office of Education in Washington, D. C., would tend unduly to jeopardize the rightful control by states and local communities over their own education.

( ) ( ) ( ) 52. The scholastic attainments of pupils as revealed by standardized achievement tests constitute a reliable basis upon which to rate the teachers of those pupils.

( ) ( ) ( ) 53. The success of exact science in achieving control and mastery of mechanical things is an indication of what may be expected when the methods of the exact sciences are applied to the fields of human and social phenomena.

( ) ( ) ( ) 54. It is misleading to believe that any one is a "born teacher."

( ) ( ) ( ) 55. I believe that it is *often* desirable to subordinate the good in the child's present living to the greater good of his future adult life.

( ) ( ) ( ) 56. To think of motive as a part of the act performed is truer than to think of motive as back of and impelling the act performed.

( ) ( ) ( ) 57. Education may well be conceived as the unfolding of what is latent in the child.

( ) ( ) ( ) 58. The school will fail to measure up to its responsibilities in reducing crime in the degree that it gives up its well established principles of discipline to make way for greater pupil freedom.

( ) ( ) ( ) 59. The individual is born with a mind which serves him throughout life as an agent for acquiring and retaining knowledge.

( ) ( ) ( ) 60. Environmental influences, more than heredity, determine the differences in mental ability which children show.

( ) ( ) ( ) 61. To believe that the spirit of man, like his body, is simply a part of nature is to deny him the possibility of enjoying the finer things in life.

( ) ( ) ( ) 62. Mind is individual; that is, each person has his own mind which is not only distinct from the minds of all other persons, but is also set apart from the world to be known.

( ) ( ) ( ) 63. The people of some nations possess on the average a greater native capacity for learning languages than do the people of some other nations.

( ) ( ) ( ) 64. In teaching such subjects as geography and history, I favor the following procedure: pretest, teach, test the result, adapt the procedure, teach and test again to the point of actual learning.

( ) ( ) ( ) 65. In man's experience there are two realms: one an inner, characterized by mind; the other an outer, characterized by mere physical activity.

( ) ( ) ( ) 66. Man's inborn tendency to fight makes it highly improbable that war can ever be entirely abolished.

( ) ( ) ( ) 67. Educational experts rather than class-room teachers should make the curriculum.

( ) ( ) ( ) 68. I consider that man has a two-fold nature, consisting of body and soul.

( ) ( ) ( ) 69. As far as capacity for education is concerned, one race is practically as capable of higher civilization as another.

( ) ( ) ( ) 70. Children from the first school years on, should be given a genuine determining part in selecting the activities of their school curriculum.

( ) ( ) ( ) 71. To say that an individual has a soul is only to call attention to certain characteristics of his ways of feeling and acting as a human organism.

( ) ( ) ( ) 72. Classes in society are determined largely by conditions which are biologically inherent, hence social stratification must be accepted in any social order.

( ) ( ) ( ) 73. Coercion is necessary in schools because a good curriculum must call for the learning of many things whose value the young pupil cannot yet appreciate.

( ) ( ) ( ) 74. It is more true to say that the self *is* the habits acquired by the individual in the course of his life than to say that the self must be there to acquire the habits.

( ) ( ) ( ) 75. The source of economic competition is found in the trait of acquisitiveness in man's original nature.

( ) ( ) ( ) 76. Man's faculty of reason is complete in itself apart from the subject matter upon which man applies his reason.

( ) ( ) ( ) 77. Moral principles come from a source outside ourselves, and as such should be the determiners of changing social conditions rather than determined by them.

( ) ( ) ( ) 78. Orphan infants adopted into very desirable homes sometimes turn out disappointingly. I consider that in most such cases original nature is probably a more potent factor than environment.

( ) ( ) ( ) 79. The dominance of the white race in the world today bespeaks a mental capacity superior to that of other races.

A SOCIAL STUDY*
By Manly H. Harper, Ph.D.

DIRECTIONS
A. Filling the Blanks Below (omitted)
B. Marking the Propositions of the Study

Before turning to mark the following three pages of propositions please read these directions carefully.

In plans for the development of good citizenship full weight and proper consideration should be given to the opinions and ideals of teachers and other educators. Your sincere coöperation is desired, therefore, in marking the propositions of this study. Use care but do not take more time than you need. You should be able to complete the marking in 35 or, at most, 45 minutes.

If you agree with a proposition more fully than you disagree, mark it by placing a plus sign (+) in the parentheses at the left of the number.

If you disagree more fully than you agree, mark the proposition by placing a minus (—) in the parentheses at the left of the number.

Please mark each proposition even if in some cases you feel that you are merely guessing.

Make sure that you understand the above directions in the blackface type.

THE PROPOSITIONS

( ) 1. In teaching the vital problems of citizenship, teachers should so impress on the students the approved opinions in these matters that life's later experiences can never unsettle or modify the opinions given.

( ) 2. If our people were willing to try the experiment fairly the government ownership of railroads would be for the best interests of the country.

( ) 3. The practice of democracy, as developed in the United States, has no serious or far-reaching defects.

( ) 4. As a rule, the laborer in this country has as favorable an opportunity to obtain a fair price for his labor as his employer has to obtain a fair price for the goods which the laborer produces.

( ) 5. One should never allow his own experience and reason to lead him in ways that he knows are contrary to the teachings of the Bible.

( ) 6. The government should provide to all classes of people opportunity for insurance at cost against accident, sickness, premature death, and old age.

( ) 7. For the improvement of patriotism our laws should forbid much of the radical criticism that we often hear and read concerning the injustice of our country and government.

( ) 8. If any facts should be found favorable to socialism they should be omitted from histories written for high school use.

( ) 9. Among the poor, many more individuals fall short of highest satisfaction on account of too many desires than on account of lack of income.

( ) 10. The United States should exercise a wider and firmer control in Latin America.

( ) 11. Very large fortunes gained in this country have, in almost all cases, been obtained by proportionately large service to the common welfare.

( ) 12. The United States is justified in refusing to join the League of Nations.

( ) 13. Licenses to teach in the public school should be refused to persons believing in socialism.

( ) 14. The measure of right or wrong in human action is in direct proportion to the measure in which the action enriches or impoverishes human experience.

( ) 15. On the whole in this country, the reward given manual laborers, as

* Published and copyrighted, 1927, by Teachers College, Columbia University. *First printed in 1922 for private use in research. Revised Edition printed 1930.*

compared with the share taken by their employers, has been in just proportion to the services they have rendered.

( ) 16. The United States should avoid any extensive program of government ownership and operation in the generation, transmission, and distribution of hydroelectric power.

( ) 17. The present curricula of our schools are well suited to the development of broad and sympathetic understanding among our various economic groups—farmers, miners, manufacturers, etc.

( ) 18. During the dangers of impending war our government should prevent any groups of citizens from opposing, through public discussions or through publications, the government's most thorough preparation for the possible conflict.

( ) 19. Without directly teaching religion a teacher's influence in the public schools should always be definitely and positively favorable to the purposes and activities of our generally recognized religious organizations.

( ) 20. The wage system of industry operates with desirable efficiency in promoting the interest of laborers in the work they are employed to do.

( ) 21. Some events in the history of the United States during the past 40 years show that influential groups among our people have at times swayed our government into imperialism, the selfish policy of controlling and exploiting the people of another nation.

( ) 22. Because of conditions developed by science and invention, nations that continue to grow in strength and justice will inevitably become less interdependent.

( ) 23. Most students of our high schools should give a larger proportion of their time to the study of ancient languages, in view of the benefit of general mental development and refinement to be derived therefrom.

( ) 24. Our generally recognized religious organizations retard progress by continuing to operate as the dead hand of the past, hindering, through subservience to mythical superhuman authority, efficient search for truth and justice.

( ) 25. No normally healthy individual can justly appropriate and enjoy more property than he has earned by service to the common good.

( ) 26. The development of the highest welfare of the country will require government ownership of important minerals.

( ) 27. World conditions seem now to insure enduring peace among the nations.

( ) 28. In the industries of this country proper opportunity and encouragement are usually given to laborers to progress from lower to higher positions of all grades of responsibility and reward.

( ) 29. The methods and curricula now commonly employed in teaching citizenship insure our country's efficient progress in democracy.

( ) 30. Our educational forces should be directed toward a more thoroughly socialistic order of society.

( ) 31. For the sake of our continued prosperity teachers should endeavor to give students of suitable age a firm understanding of and belief in the protective tariff policy.

( ) 32. Many more industries and parts of industries should be owned and operated coöperatively by the producers (all the workers) themselves.

( ) 33. The power of huge fortunes in this country endangers democracy.

( ) 34. In the elementary schools a direct study of the Constitution of the United States has greater possibilities for building citizenship than has any study or work that can be properly undertaken in the practical arts— such as home-making, agriculture, mining, manufacturing, etc.

( ) 35. Events since the World War have shown clearly that the permanent policy of the United States should be to let Europe settle its political problems without our government's participation.

( ) 36. Considering the present lack of respect for authority, teachers should rise to the occasion by depending less on the self-direction of students and more on the firmly enforced plans and directions given by the teacher.

( ) 37. As a rule, the time spent on Latin by the girls in our high schools could much better be spent on such subjects as music, fine arts, home-making, literature, or social studies.

( ) 38. Some form of public regulation of business or some form of taxation should be used that would make impossible the accumulation or holding of a fortune as large as some fortunes now held.

( ) 39. Reproduction should be made impossible, by segregation or by surgical operation, for all those below certain low standards of physical and mental fitness.

( ) 40. Teachers can get no practical help from psychology that cannot be better obtained from mere common sense experience.

( ) 41. On the whole, we have had too much of government interference or regulation in private business.

( ) 42. The history of protective tariff legislation in this country is a worthy record of our government's impartial and efficient devotion to the welfare of all the people.

( ) 43. It should become common practice for owners of capital to share profits and management with their employees.

( ) 44. A large majority of those who usually vote the Republican ticket are influenced in their voting more by ignorance and prejudice than by rational thought. (No comparison with other parties is implied.)

( ) 45. Every boy and girl in American schools should be taught to give unquestioning and unlimited respect and support to the American flag.

( ) 46. History shows no development to encourage the hope that there can ever be a practical international or world government to deal with international or world affairs.

( ) 47. Our radical papers exaggerate greatly when they say that 5 per cent of our population owns 95 per cent of all the property in this country.

( ) 48. The development of the highest welfare of the country will require government ownership of the land.

( ) 49. The members of Congress from the agricultural sections should coöperate to make the laws of greatest possible advantage to the farmers.

( ) 50. There is no probability that the means of forming public opinion (especially the schools and the press) will be unfairly influenced or controlled by the wealthy interests.

( ) 51. Any self-direction by students of the elementary school should be limited to routine matters and special projects, leaving the regular work to be planned and directed entirely by the teacher.

( ) 52. We should attempt to give students in our public schools an abiding faith in the Constitution of the United States in all its parts and principles.

( ) 53. No school, college, or university should teach anything that is found to result in its students doubting or questioning the Bible as containing the word of God.

( ) 54. If every nation were as wise and just as the United States there would be no danger of more great wars.

( ) 55. In these days of lack of thoroughness, elementary teachers should give their attention more singly and directly to teaching the fundamentals—in reading, handwriting, arithmetic, etc.

( ) 56. The only god we should serve is truth revealed through the interpretation of experience by clear, unselfish, rational thought.

( ) 57. In matters of citizenship the student's interests, mental attitudes, and methods of work are not so vital as his desire to remember the conclusions emphasized by the teacher and other qualified authorities.

( ) 58. Our laws should prohibit giving information, even to adults, concerning birth control, through public meetings or through the mails.

( ) 59. By legislative and executive action, government in this country has often given manufacturing and commercial interests special advantages seriously detrimental to other important interests.

( ) 60. The man whose vacant lots in a thriving city increase many fold in value because the city's homes and business grow up around those lots, should, in justice, be required to repay in taxes a large part of the unearned profits to the city that created the increased values.

( ) 61. A league or association of nations, including the United States, is the only kind of organization sufficiently inclusive to deal adequately with broader international affairs.

( ) 62. The opportunities for education offered to the young of this country show that our people are properly sensitive and loyal to the principle of equality of opportunity for all.

( ) 63. A larger proportion of time in our high schools should be given to such subjects as modern history, civics, economics, and sociology.

( ) 64. If it were true that 1 per cent of the citizens of the United States owned more property than the other 99 per cent, it would be of great importance in our high schools to seek to interest the students in a study of the causes operating to produce this unequal distribution of wealth.

( ) 65. Citizens should desire our elementary and high schools to give unprejudiced and vigorous study and discussion to important social and political issues upon which community opinion is divided.

( ) 66. It would be undemocratic for the United States to surrender any of its sovereign power to an international super-government in order to become a member of such an organization.

( ) 67. Taxes on very large inheritances should be high enough to prevent any heirs receiving huge fortunes.

( ) 68. The classroom teacher should be given a larger and more responsible share in organizing the curriculum of the school and in determining the subject matter and method of her own teaching.

( ) 69. It would be well to give a larger proportion of the time in our elementary schools to elements involved in the problems of capital and labor.

( ) 70. Histories written for elementary or high school use should omit any facts likely to arouse in the minds of the students questions or doubt concerning the justice of our social order and government.

( ) 71. The life and work of the school cannot properly be like the activities of life outside of school because the school has its own work to do in preparing young people for later life.